AMERICA'S COACH

Life Lessons & Wisdom for Gold Medal Success;
A Biographical Journey of the Late Hockey Icon Herb Brooks

by
Ross Bernstein

Best Wishes Chris !

Ross Bernstein

1-24-13

AMERICA'S COACH
Life Lessons & Wisdom for Gold Medal Success;
A Biographical Journey of the Late Hockey Icon Herb Brooks
by
Ross Bernstein

Self-Published by Bernstein Books, L.L.C.

WWW.BERNSTEINBOOKS.COM

ISBN: 0-9634871-9-1

Photos courtesy of: the Brooks family, University of Minnesota,
St. Cloud State University, New York Rangers & USA Hockey

Printed by Printing Enterprises, New Brighton, MN • (651) 636-9336

*A portion of the proceeds from the sale of this book will
benefit the Herb Brooks Foundation. Thank you for your
support in giving the game back to the kids!*

WWW.HERBBROOKSFOUNDATION.COM

THE HERB BROOKS FOUNDATION

The Herb Brooks Foundation is dedicated to providing more opportunities for kids to play the game of hockey. True to his words, the Foundation will assist in "making hockey fun for kids and letting them learn to love the game the way we did." In keeping with this ideal, the Foundation will support programs that emphasize the development of youth hockey players and coaches throughout the country. The Foundation will also assist in providing more outdoor hockey facilities and programs, which directly impact the development of youth hockey players.

Brooks' legacy and vision will be celebrated in 2007 when the Herb Brooks Arena and Training Center is opened at the National Sports Center in Blaine, Minn. The facility, a state-of-the-art 12,000 square foot educational center, will truly change the game for countless young boys and girls who want to play the game of hockey the right way, with respect.

The Herb Brooks Foundation will become the "cornerstone" in the effort to "grow" the sport of ice hockey – a hockey future that will improve the skill level of American players to world-class status. This will be done by teaching and showing players, parents, officials, coaches and youth associations "by example" how to make hockey less structured and more fun while helping build the base of the pyramid. This method will increase the number of kids playing and increase their skill level at the same time. The Foundation will be widely recognized as an innovator, providing a place where players, parents, officials and coaches share a common vision and sense of what is really important for our youth playing hockey and other sports.

Furthermore, the Foundation will establish an awards celebration at its annual Herb Brooks Foundation Awards Banquet; an internet based Minnesota Youth Hockey Hall of Fame; and explore the possibility of developing a future sports academy and prep school. In addition, the Herb Brooks award is given annually to the most qualified hockey player in the Minnesota State High School Hockey Tournament who strongly represents the values, characteristics, and traits that defined the award's namesake.

FOR INFORMATION OR TO MAKE A DONATION:

Herb Brooks Foundation
National Sports Center
1700 105th Ave. N.E.
Blaine, MN 55449

WWW.HERBBROOKSFOUNDATION.COM

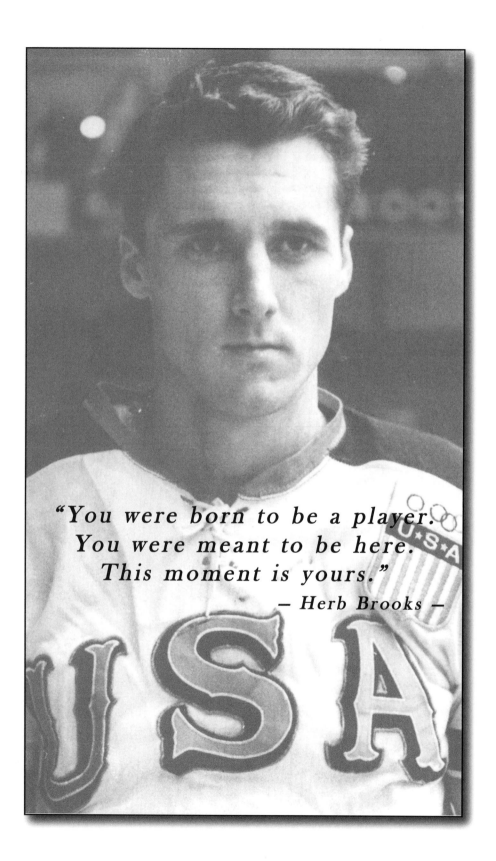

"You were born to be a player.
You were meant to be here.
This moment is yours."
— Herb Brooks —

TABLE OF CONTENTS

FOREWORD BY JIM CRAIG

We never have enough mentors, especially hardworking, smart, experienced, and passionate mentors. A mentor affects change forever; he does this through the people he educates and drives and inspires, each of whom, in turn, teach and pass on to others his lessons, guidance and motivation.

Mentors believe in dreams, and convince others to believe in those dreams, to buy in to those dreams.

We all can benefit from a mentor.

We can benefit from a mentor no matter how old we are or how much experience we have. A mentor can help us improve no matter if we are already exceptional at what we do or merely ordinary. Whether we possess loads of natural talent or not much at all, a mentor can make us better.

Mentors seek to teach, guide, and inspire their students to reach their potential – to reach their potential on the ice rink and football field, the classroom and laboratory, the halls of justice and seats of government, and the boardroom and executive offices.

Mentors tutor, push, pull, cajole, agitate, and provoke their students to search within themselves and find the seeds and stuff of talent, sometimes greatness, and maybe – even if only rarely – magic.

Mentors strive to transmit to their students a healthy understanding of priorities and responsibility and values.

Herb Brooks was a mentor.

Herb Brooks was a great mentor.

Herb Brooks was my mentor.

In the summer of 2006 a story that I wrote on teamwork was published in the business magazine Opportunity. A considerable portion of that story discussed the influence of Herb Brooks on my life and the lives of my teammates.

Here is an excerpt from that story:

Back in the late 1800s, about 40 miles northwest of North Easton [my hometown], in the town of Concord, lived a man who wrote beautifully and put to paper, and spoke, a lot of very wise and very smart things. His name was Henry David Thoreau. "Most men live lives of quiet desperation," wrote Thoreau, "and go to the grave with the song still in them."

I think those words would have struck a chord with Coach Brooks.

You see, Coach Brooks was not going to have any team, ever, that lived and played in quiet desperation. He also was not going to coach players who would leave anything on the ice, who would become old men and wonder what could have been, who would lament not daring greatly, and who would pass from this world not having exercised their gifts and given their all.

If you played for Herb Brooks, you were going to prepare, practice, and train ...and prepare, practice, and train ... and prepare, practice, and train ... again and again and again.

You would be ready.

The strategies and tactics that Coach Brooks employed did not always sit well with us. More often than not, his way of doing things got us grumbling and irritated.

A good portion of the time what he said to us and how he pushed us made us boil with anger.

That was fine with Coach Brooks. He wasn't there to pacify or play up to us, to solicit our affection, or to stroke our egos. He was there to make us winners.

For years, Coach Brooks had chased a dream and worked, risked, and sacrificed to be in position to realize that dream – to build just the right team, to prepare that team, and to coach that team the night that it executed the almost perfect game of hockey.

Playing nice and being our buddy could wait.

As well, Coach Brooks correctly reasoned that a team united in its dislike of the coach would have the common enemy so vital to the character of highly functioning groups.

He hardly cared if he were that enemy.

In his New York Times bestselling book, "The Boys of Winter: The Untold Story of a Coach, a Dream, and the 1980 U.S. Olympic Team," Wayne Coffey described the influence that Coach Brooks had on me.

"Herb Brooks constantly prodded him and goaded him and made him feel uncomfortable," wrote Coffey. "Craig, didn't always like it, but it made him a better person. It taught him to take risks and dream big."

Yes, Coach Brooks rode me, challenged me, and got on my case, over and over. He rode my teammates, challenged them, and got on their case, over and over. But Coach Brooks was even-handed and fair; his rule and discipline were evenly applied.

Green Bay Packer great and NFL Hall of Fame lineman Henry Jordan said that his coach, the legendary Vince Lombardi, treated every member of the Packer team the same – "like dogs."

In a Sports Illustrated story that commemorated the 25th anniversary of the Miracle on Ice, the author of the story, E.M. Swift, noted that every member of our team said that "rotten" was the way Coach Brooks treated him.

Yet, for sure, even though Coach Brooks was tough, gruff, and demanding, he understood what all exceptional mentors understand: praise and encouragement has its place, and is especially valuable when parsed out sparingly and in reward for truly high dedication and achievement.

When Coach Brooks dispensed a kind word and pat on the back, it really meant something, and it carried with it a special capacity to energize and rouse us.

Coach Brooks also appreciated the pressure his players faced, and under which we trained and competed. Indeed, his Spartan system and methods conditioned us to handle the pressure. As the games approached, and during the Olympic tournament itself, Coach Brooks put himself in the spotlight and shielded us from the media. He did this not to grab glory, not to take from us recognition we deserved, but rather to protect us from unnerving and distracting influences, and to keep us focused.

He dreamed for us – and made his dream our dream. It became a shared dream.

That dream took us all the way to a date with history on an ice rink in upstate New York.

In the locker room prior our epic meeting with the Soviet Union, Coach Brooks, in character, as always, said to us sternly and confidently, "You were born a player. You were meant to be here at this time. This moment is yours."

We believed him. Because of the way he had taught and treated and tested us – the way he had mentored us – we were sure that Coach Brooks spoke the truth.

And because he spoke the truth, what happened later that evening became possible.

Herb Brooks meant so much to the sport of hockey. He touched countless people over the years from all levels of the game and from all walks of life. Everybody who has ever played for him has taken something from him, whether it was his honesty; his work ethic; his discipline; his love and passion for the sport; or his practical lessons which applied to everyday life.

For me, the biggest things that I took from him were honesty and hard work. He told you exactly where he stood on things and was always straight forward with you. His work ethic, meanwhile, was like nothing I had ever seen before. I would like to think that some of those qualities rubbed off on me and how I lead my own life today.

Herb taught me about commitment and about the desire and passion it takes to achieve your goals. You know, I have never met anybody who is successful in life because they are lucky. People are successful because they work hard and prepare, and those were the cornerstones of Herb's philosophy for success.

With regards to his legacy, it will be many things to many people. Sure, the "Miracle on Ice" will always be linked to him, but it is really much, much more than that. Through his love and passion for teaching, he was able to grow and expand the game to truly make it a national sport. And, because of his loyalty towards American players, the game was able to prosper in a way it had never done so before. The U.S. kids needed opportunities at that time and thanks to people like Herb Brooks, they got them.

The 1980 team really opened up the eyes of the nation to the sport of hockey and that was a big deal. The game prior to that had mostly been regional, in the north and east, but that all changed when we won the gold medal in such a dramatic fashion. The game expanded to the south and west shortly thereafter and I am convinced that a lot of the credit for that should be given to Herb. He had a vision and he had a plan. Not only did he want to win the gold medal and make his country proud, he also wanted to grow the game the right way, starting at the youth levels and building it up from there.

One of the things I am most proud of is the fact that since the movie "Miracle" came out a few years ago, countless high school, college and professional teams from around the world of sports have watched it in preparation of their "big games." That is so neat. I mean to have been a small part of such an uplifting, inspirational story about dreams and determination is unbelievable. We just had a great group of players with the right makeup of character and values, who were brought together from very diverse backgrounds. Our common denominator, however, was Herb, and he was able to instill in us a style of hockey that was innovative, creative and emotional.

He reminded us to play the game with passion and with respect. He let us know that each of us had a role and that that role was vital towards the overall success of the team. We were a group of young men who came together with a unified goal and through a lot of hard work and unselfishness, we accomplished our dreams and made history in the process. So, to know that other young people are inspired by our achievements, makes me very proud.

I also know that Herb was in the game for all the right reasons. He wanted to coach and to teach and to win. He didn't care about the glory or recognition, that wasn't what he was all about. For him, it was about getting his players to perform at their very best on a given night in order to achieve what most felt at the time was impossible. He took the pressure off of us, as a team, by putting the focus on him instead. It was always "us against him" and he brought us together that way, to build our chemistry and character.

Yes, there was a method to his madness and as a motivator, the man was a genius. It wasn't about Mike Eruzione or about Jim Craig or even about Herb Brooks though, it was about the 1980 U.S. Olympic hockey team. Period. It was about 20 players working together towards a common goal. The fact that Herb walked off the ice after we won the gold medal just proved that he was true to his word. He felt like that was our time and he wanted us to share it together while he stood quietly in the background. At that point the job was done in his eyes. He had prepared us and we went out and did the work. As a result, he let us enjoy the fruits of our labor. That's the kind of guy he was.

I think he and I got along well from the start because we both came from similar backgrounds. Even though I was a Boston kid, and there was an intense rivalry there, believe me, he gave me a shot and I will forever be grateful for that. He liked the "lunch pail - hard hat" players who were tough, and I would like to think that that was me to a tee. We were both blue collar guys whose parents worked hard so that their kids could have opportunities that they didn't. We were also both underdogs too, and because of that I think we could relate on a different level.

The fact that we became friends later in life meant the world to me too. He had always been very stand-offish with his players, so it was a friendship and mentorship that was extremely special to me. When Herb was inducted into the U.S. Hockey Hall of Fame, he asked me to be his presenter and I was completely honored. Then, when Patti and Danny and Kelly asked me to speak at his funeral, I was completely humbled. What great people and what a great family. That, more than anything, is the legacy I am sure Herb is most proud of.

Herb taught me that if you are willing to work hard for something and you believe in it, then you can accomplish anything. He was a great coach, a great family man and a great person. I am proud to say that he was my friend. I really miss him and I know that the entire sport of hockey really misses him too. He was a real American hero.

Do You Believe in Miracles?...YES!

Those words still give me goose bumps every time I hear them. They take me back to when I was just a 10-year-old kid living in the sleepy southern Minnesota town of Fairmont, just a few miles from the Iowa border. Hockey country it wasn't. Nope. No indoor arena; no zamboni; not even any matching uniforms; nada. It was pretty bleak.

That all changed in the Winter of 1980 though, when the U.S. Olympic hockey team shocked the word in Lake Placid, NY. I wasn't even a hockey fan at the time, but as soon as I started watching those games on TV, I was hooked. Seeing them beat the seemingly invincible Soviets, arguably the greatest hockey team ever assembled, was simply magical. Then, to watch them rally back to beat the Finns two days later to win the gold medal, it truly was a "Miracle on Ice." For me, that was it. I immediately went out to our local Coast to Coast Hardware store in the downtown plaza and bought a used pair of Bauer Hugger skates. I wanted in.

Little did I know at that very moment, however, was that I was about to embark on the journey of a lifetime that would ultimately bring me full-circle more than a quarter century later. Believe it or not, that single event would have an impact on my life all these years later that I never could have dreamed of. Was it destiny? I don't know. But whatever it was, it had a hold of me and would consume me over the ensuing years like nothing I had ever known before. You see, that passion for the sport of hockey which I discovered back then would eventually lead me to the coach of that Icy Miracle, Herb Brooks, and wind up serving as the genesis behind this book.

I got to meet Coach Brooks just a few months later at his Summer hockey camp in nearby Faribault, at Shattuck Military Academy. I begged my parents to let me sign up and they reluctantly agreed. There, I was what you would call an "ankle bender." You know, one of *those* kid who could barely stand up. Herb took the time to say hi to me though and encouraged me to keep working hard. It certainly wasn't a long conversation, that was for sure, but at the time it meant the world to me and really inspired me to keep at it. I remember being in awe of him. I also remember being scared to death of him too. And do you know what? Those first impressions of the man who I thought was larger than life would never change, even 25 years later.

My family moved to a new house on Hall Lake that year and I would now have all the ice time I could ask for, weather permitting of course. Now, as for organized hockey? That was a different story. The local school's didn't sponsor us or even recognize us for that matter, so it was up to the parents to get things done. Youth hockey programs in places like Fairmont were completely grass roots operations. We had just the bare necessities: an outdoor rink, a warming house, and a couple of shovels to keep us busy between periods. Everybody pitched in as volunteers; from my coach, who was also my dentist; to my mom, who sold brownies at the concession stand.

I remember sticking around after practices late at night to help flood the rink out in the bitter cold. Some of my fondest childhood memories would take place out there though, at old Cardinal Park, with some of my closest friends even to this day. My parents would drop me off out there on a Saturday or Sunday morning and then pick me up late that night. I loved it. Sure, it was freezing, but we didn't care. We came inside only to warm up our toes and to snag a piece of Jake's Pizza, if one of my buddies' moms was nice enough to bring some over for us.

Ironically, as I would later learn, it wasn't that much different from how Herb Brooks learned the game out on the frozen ponds of St. Paul's east side. He used to talk about those days with a big smile on his face. Those were, in his eyes, "the days." And, the fact that kids don't grow up in those environments anymore, fueled his desire to grow the game from "the base of the pyramid up," as he used to say. Herb wanted to get more kids playing outdoors, where they could be creative and have fun without having to worry about coaches or parents yelling or screaming at them. He wanted to give the game back to the kids, and he knew that started with getting them more "structured, unstructured ice time" at places like Cardinal Park.

I made it through squirts, then peewees and bantams. As a freshman in high school I found myself as a starting defenseman on the varsity. No, it's not what you're thinking. I didn't get really good over that time and emerge as some hot-shot phenom. Remember, this was Fairmont, and there was a serious need for warm bodies. Big games for us were against other southern Minnesota powerhouses such as Marshall, Windom, Sleepy Eye and Worthington. Occasionally, we would play Mankato or Austin, and that would usually result in a tough lesson in humility, followed by a long ride home. We didn't even have school jerseys, Dominos Pizza sponsored us instead. There were no locker rooms or fancy busses either, just the bathroom at McDonald's on the way home. The key was to get a ride with one of the players' whose parents owned a van, where you could stretch out on the way home. If you got stuck in a pick-up truck, you would have to spend at least 15 minutes thawing out your frozen skates when you got there.

I played through high school and had a blast. I then went on to attend the University of Minnesota in 1987. My entire family had gone to the U and I was excited to be a Gopher. There, I became buddies with a few of the Gopher hockey players through my fraternity and eventually they encouraged me to try out as a walk-on. The Gophers had a junior varsity in those days and I figured that if I could just make the JV, then that would be about the pinnacle of my playing career. From there, I could always fantasize about a "Rudy" type moment in which I would get thrown out for one varsity shift as a fifth-year senior during a ten-nothing blow-out over Alabama-Huntsville. Hey, a guy can dream. I was a huge Gopher fan at the time and even had season tickets to watch them play at old Mariucci Arena. So, I just went for it. Nothing ventured; nothing gained was how I saw it.

It turned out to be a great experience. I pretty much did what I was told and stayed under the radar as a practice pylon. The end came when I tried to impress the coaches by checking one of the team's star players, Todd Richards, who was injured at the time and rehabbing with the JV. I remember he was wearing a white jersey with a big red cross on it, and he came skating right towards me with his head down. Now was my chance to make an impression I thought, so I nailed him. It was a great hit.

At that point things get fuzzy, because shortly thereafter Bill Butters, an assistant coach and former NHL tough-guy, ran me over like road kill. When I regained consciousness, I was reminded that players with red crosses were injured and not to be touched. It was a lesson learned the hard way, unfortunately, because it wasn't long afterwards that I was graciously shown the door. Apparently Coach Woog wouldn't be needing my services after all.

After my brief "cup of coffee," however, it came to my attention that there was another job opening within the program that might be more suitable to my talents: the team mascot, "Goldy Gopher." There were two criteria for the position: you had to be a decent skater; and you had to be a complete fool. I Apparently fit on both accounts and got the gig. I still wanted to be a part of the team and this was going to be the perfect opportunity to do just that.

Being Goldy was so much fun. I got to be an anonymous entertainer up on the old TV perch under the scoreboard at the Old Barn. The Gophers seldom if ever lost during those days at home, which made my job a lot easier too. I got to still hang out with the team and take part in practices too, which was just fantastic. Eventually a publisher approached me and told me he was interested in writing a book about all of the antics that I had gotten into as a mischievous rodent. From bowling over opposing cheerleader pyramids at center ice; to messing with unsuspecting referees; to dropping my props, Gumby and Pokey, onto the ice from high above my perch and getting delay of game penalties for my home team; I certainly got into my fair share of trouble, no question. I told him I was flattered, but no thanks. Then, as I was finishing my last year of school, I thought about doing my own book about the program's rich history. Only I would write it from Goldy's perspective instead. I had no business writing a book, but really didn't want to enter the real world at that point either. So, I took a leap of faith and decided to self-publish what would turn out to be my first book, entitled appropriately enough: *"Gopher Hockey by the Hockey Gopher."*

It would exceed my wildest expectations and even turn out to be a regional best-seller. Who knew? The book wound up as a history of the program as told through the eyes of hundreds of former players, coaches and media personalities. I bought a tape recorder and just started interviewing people. I wasn't going to be winning any Pulitzers, that was for sure, but the Maroon and Gold faithful were thrilled that something was finally going to be written about their beloved Gophers. They wanted to read about the behind the scenes stuff and then laugh out loud to all of the funny stories.

A few months into the project, I got a call one day from none other than Herb Brooks. He was coaching with the New Jersey Devils at the time, but had heard about what I was doing and wanted to help me out. I was floored. I mean this guy was *IT* for me and I couldn't believe he had actually called me. And he couldn't have been more gracious with his time, I will never forget it. He told me that he had heard about my project and that he thought it was great. We talked for more than an hour. Herb knew that I was doing something historic and he respected that. He knew that I was paying homage to guys like John Mariucci, his old coach, and that in his eyes, I was all right.

He also told me that he liked the fact that even though I wasn't good enough to play Gopher hockey, that I still wanted to be a part of Gopher hockey. Herb was all about growing the game and I think he saw in me a young guy who was ripe to be recruited for his cause. He was right. Incredibly, that would be the beginning of a very special relationship I would have with Herb, which would grow and manifest over the ensuing decade or so.

After graduating, I got married and wound up spending the next several years living in both Chicago and New York. I eventually moved home in 1996 though, to pursue my dream of becoming a full-time sports author. I immediately jumped into a new coffee table book project that year about Minnesota's greatest sports heroes, and of course, one of the first people I called was Herb. I would chronicle his story in several more books as the years went by, and each time I grew to understand him a little bit more. Later, when I served as the editor of a local hockey magazine, we would talk frequently about various issues which he felt strongly about. I learned pretty quickly to listen carefully and to always come prepared. Going to see Herb was like going to see the principal; he could be pretty intense and intimidating at times.

He could also be very deep and very compassionate too, which was the other side of the glacier-like facade that surrounded him. You just did not want to disappoint him. He was an extremely passionate person and was so strong about his convictions; letting him down was usually not an option. While I was never a part of his inner circle, that was a place reserved for a select few, I was someone he grew to trust when it came to writing and publishing. So, when he called me in the Fall of 2002 to ask me to write a series of motivational books with him, I was absolutely blown away.

You see, Herb had recently turned down a multi-million dollar contract to come back to New York and coach the struggling Rangers.

He had decided that at the age of 65 he wanted to spend the next chapter of his life with his kids and grandkids, something he missed out on a lot of the time the first time around. So, he respectfully said no. His new plan was to be a full-time grandpa and a part-time motivational speaker on the national circuit. As a speaker, he was one of the best in the business. He commanded big bucks and was highly sought after by executives from Fortune 500 companies from coast to coast. What he needed, however, were some books to tie into his presentation. This is where my story comes full circle.

He had told me that there were several big name writers in the mix that he had considered for the job, guys from ESPN and such, but that he wanted to go with someone he knew and trusted. He wanted to go with an underdog, a little guy, and give me a break; which was something he was always known for. He said I had earned that. I was thrilled for the opportunity and was determined to make the most of it. Career-wise, it was going to be a big feather in my cap to be able to work hand in hand with the legendary Herb Brooks. Not many people get to work with their idols in their lifetime, and I knew it was a hallmark moment for me.

With that, the phone calls increased and so did the preparations. One thing I learned right out of the gates working with Herb Brooks was that the man was extremely organized and meticulously prepared for anything and everything that came his way. Herb also liked to surround himself with "experts" in things he wanted to learn about. Whether it was breaking down the Russian version of the neutral zone trap; learning to plant a new variety of hostas; building a new deck; or writing a book; he was never too proud to ask for help and that was one of the reasons I believe why he was so successful.

I eventually set up some meetings with some publishers and literary agents, but it soon became apparent that he wanted to do things his own way. So, we decided that we were going to publish the books ourselves, which would give Herb total control over the finished product — something that was obviously very important to him. Under this scenario, I was going to serve as his author, publicist and personal assistant. Looking back, I clearly had no idea what I was getting myself into at that point, but we marched ahead nonetheless.

We would spend the next six months working on and off the book project. As things would come up, he would switch the book from the front burner to the back burner, always changing things as we went along. Herb had a difficult time making decisions though, and the project soon began to take on a life of its own. It would evolve from books and speaking engagements, to the possibility of creating a magazine, as well as TV and radio shows. He had a lot of ideas on how he wanted to change the game at that particular juncture of his life, especially at the youth levels, and wanted a large platform to preach from. He had a lot of clout and was clearly somebody who could get things like that done if he really wanted to. The problem was just being able to pull the trigger.

Another exciting component to the entire project was the fact that he had been working with Disney that Summer on the movie "Miracle," which would feature actor Kurt Russell as Herb. He knew that when the movie hit the screens that Winter, the book sales would take off like wild fire. More phone calls and meetings ensued, as did revised outlines, sample chapters and media plans. And let me tell you, phone calls with Herb Brooks were not short. They could go on for hours. He just loved to talk; and quite frankly, I loved to listen. By mid-Summer things were heating up and it was getting really exciting.

Flash forward to the weekend of August 11th. Herb had been asked to play in the U.S. Hockey Hall of Fame Celebrity Golf Classic, up at Giant's Ridge Golf Course in Biwabik, Minn. Herb was an inductee of the Hall of Fame and was always willing to help them out and do his part to promote the growth of American hockey. Plus, he loved that particular golf course and was really looking forward to spending the weekend with some of his dearest friends up on the Iron Range.

So, he drove up for the weekend and attended a fundraiser for the Eveleth Hippodrome on that first night, Saturday. He then spent that evening at former teammate and longtime friend John Mayasich's cabin on nearby Lake Esquagama. He and the boys would golf 18 holes on Sunday and then partake in the Hall of Fame dinner festivities that night which honored both Bobby and Brett Hull. Brett, of course, had just played for Brooks as a member of the 2002 Olympic team, and he was looking forward to catching up with him. It was a great situation for Herb to be in because he wasn't required to speak or to receive any awards that evening, he was just there to have fun — a real rarity for him.

After the dinner I had a beer with Herb and we talked about the book. He was having a good time and was enjoying talking to all of the different people there. I eventually went back to my hotel room to hit the sack around midnight. I saw Herb that next morning during break-fast at the lodge and then again out on the driving range. Herb was tired from all of the socializing, but in a good mood. It was going to be a great day for golf. The tournament was set up in a scramble format, and all of the golf carts were lined up waiting for the signal to head off to their respective holes for a shotgun start.

He sat patiently in his cart that morning, waiting with all of the other anxious golfers to get going. For many, it was their first time play-ing the "Quarry," the second and newest course at Giant's Ridge, which had just recently opened. To pass the time, Herb was giving some of the guys a few pointers about their golf swings. He used to always hound me to keep my arm straight during my back-swing. It drove him, and me, nuts. That was Herb, always coaching, no matter what the circumstances or situation. Finally, the starter signaled for everybody to take off, the fes-tivities had officially begun. I wished him well and said good bye, I too was looking forward to hitting the links. Herb was eager to get going because he knew that he would have to leave the tournament early. He had a speaking engagement that evening in Chicago and he needed to get home in order to let the dog out and then get to the airport to catch his flight.

Finally, after 11 holes, Herb had to say his good byes to the fellas. It had been a great day, but he had to honor his prior commitments. With that, he headed back to his minivan and took off for the three hour or so drive home which he had made countless times before. He would pass through Eveleth, the birthplace of American hockey, followed by another hockey hot-bed, Cloquet, and then onto I-35 south, which would guide him to his home just north of St. Paul in White Bear Lake.

Sadly and tragically, however, he never made it home that day. On the afternoon of August 11, 2003, Herb Brooks died in a one car accident just north of the Twin Cities near the intersections of Interstates 35W and 35E, by the suburb of Forest Lake. His vehicle had veered off the road and overturned, he was killed instantly. He had just celebrated his 66th birthday that week.

By the time the tournament had ended, no one had yet heard the terrible news. I had left pretty early and drove back to my in-laws place on nearby Lake Nichols, where I spent the rest of the afternoon with my family. Then, after packing up and saying good bye, we got into our car for the trip back to the Twin Cities. As we pulled away, I turned on the radio. Immediately I could tell that something pretty big had happened, because every station was in talk mode, and their were some pretty somber discussions going on. Finally, after a few minutes of listening, I figured out what had happened. Herbie was gone. My wife and I were absolutely devastated.

We pulled over and just hugged each other for the longest time. I even hugged my dog, Herbie, who I had named in honor of my friend and mentor. We cried the whole way home, listening to caller after caller talk about what Herb Brooks had meant to them. People laughed, they cried, they told funny stories, and they all remembered Herbie. It was a surreal drive home, a day I will certainly never forget. I was just so touched by it all and really moved in a way I had never been before. I couldn't believe the impact that he had had on so many different people's lives.

Finally, after a couple of hours of driving and listening, we came upon the crash site along the highway. Police cars and news vans were still there, as were helicopters which were hovering overhead. Traffic was slowed to a crawl by that point too, as onlookers came to pay their respects to a real American hero. As we drove by, we saw a makeshift memorial that someone had made along the side of the road out of two hockey sticks in the shape of a cross, which was then draped with a Gopher jersey. I broke down at that very moment and just sobbed. I thought about how short life really is and about how lucky I was to know someone like that who had truly made a difference in this world. I felt so bad for his family and friends, I couldn't even imagine what they must have been feeling at that moment.

I think it was right then and there that I decided I too wanted to do my part to continue his legacy for the next generation of hockey fans. I thought about what I could do and the first thing that came to mind was to finish our book that we had started, only turning it into a tribute to his life instead. And that is exactly what I did. In the days and weeks following the funeral, I slowly began interviewing people close to him. I started with his wife and kids, and then went to extended family members, friends and neighbors. I then began contacting former teammates from high school, college and various Olympic teams; as well as colleagues and former players of his from the University of Minnesota, the Olympics, and the NHL teams that he coached. It was almost like coming full circle again from my first book about Gopher hockey, when I busted out my tape recorder and just started calling and interviewing.

For many I was like therapy, they were thrilled to talk about Herbie and to tell stories which would immortalize him in print. For others, however, I was like the grim reaper, coming to them to ask them about something that they didn't want to talk about. It was tough, but we all got through it. In the end, I was able to interview more than 100 people in Herbie's life and capture their raw emotions about just what he meant to them as well as to the sport of hockey. I even challenged them all by asking them in the book about what they were going to do to help carry the torch for Herbie. It turned out to be the project of a lifetime for me, it truly was. I felt like I really had made a difference.

I wanted to touch on his achievements and contributions, and then tell his story through the eyes of those who knew him best. As for the title, I went with "Remembering Herbie: Celebrating the Life & Times of Hockey Legend Herb Brooks." And that just about summed it up too, because we all just sat back and literally remembered and reminisced about someone who touched us all in some way or another. I too wanted to do my part, so I donated some of the proceeds from the book to his newly created foundation, which was all about growing the sport of hockey and giving the game back to the kids.

Over the ensuing months and years, I would be asked to speak to schools, groups and businesses about the book. They wanted to know more about this amazing person and about how he was able to manufacture the "Miracle on Ice" more than a quarter century ago up in the Adirondack Mountains of upstate New York. In so doing, I found a new meaning and purpose in my life. Thanks to the movie, "Miracle," a whole new generation of fans, many of whom "don't know the difference between a blue line and a clothes line...", have become interested in who Herb Brooks was and what he was all about. So, through my book and through speaking, I have been able to keep his legacy alive in my own small way, which is something I am extremely proud of. Herbie trusted me to tell his story and I am honored to be able to talk about the impact he had on not only my life, but on countless thousands of others as well.

Flash forward again, to the Summer of 2006. I was sitting at home one day when Kelly Paradise called, Herb's daughter. She wanted to get together to talk about doing another book about her father and if I was interested in helping her put it together. Absolutely. I was so honored that she would ask. I was thrilled to be a part of anything involving Herbie. So, after talking, I cleared my plate and immediately began working on a new book which was going to combine three unique elements of Herb's life: a biography, a motivational book, and an intimate family memoir.

We then spent the next several months assembling the pieces. Hours and hours of conversations with the family were transcribed, as were boxes and boxes of Herbie's motivational speaking notes. It was a monumental undertaking for sure, but one I was extremely excited about nonetheless. During the writing process, we eventually came to the conclusion that it was simply going to be too difficult to combine all of those components together in one package. In the end it was decided that the intimate family memoir would be better served as a stand-alone coffee table book for a later day.

So, with the blessings of Herb's wife, Patti, and his kids, Dan and Kelly, I decided to carry forward with the biography/motivational book on my own. Since *"Remembering Herbie"* was more of an anecdotal tribute book, I never really got the chance to write about a lot of the topics that Herb and I were originally working on together. And, I had always wanted to do a much more in-depth biography about him too. I just felt that this was the perfect opportunity to be able to combine both of those elements together into one package and couldn't be happier with the finished product.

As for the book itself, it was a real labor of love. Using hockey as a metaphor, I was able to weave together his life story along with his coaching philosophies and wisdom into an intricate and complex tapestry. The way I tried to write it was to take you, the reader, on a chronological journey of Herb's life, blending in many of the life lessons that I learned from him along the way, both personally and professionally. The book is filled with quotes from Herb that I had recorded and transcribed over the years from not only our unfinished book, but also from previous books and magazine articles that I had interviewed him for. I also incorporated a lot of quotes, some new and others old, from past speeches, as well as from former colleagues, players and teammates to better tell his amazing story. I in no way want to claim to be Herb's voice from the grave, rather, I want to celebrate his life in a way that is respectful to his legacy. Hopefully I achieved that goal and in the end a whole new generation of hockey fans will be able to enjoy reading about one of the true legends of the game.

Whether you want to learn about his incredible life story, or simply be inspired by the unique secrets of his success —there are plenty of great anecdotes and nuggets of inspirational wisdom in the book for you to ponder. I think that we can all learn a great deal from Herb Brooks. His unorthodox ideologies on team building, leadership and motivation are timeless. It doesn't matter if you are managing a business or trying to be a better husband, wife, mother or father, you can apply many of his practical philosophies to better your own life. Perhaps they will challenge you to find greatness in places you never dreamed possible. And maybe, just maybe, even inspire you to create your own miracles.

Looking back, the "Miracle on Ice" truly changed my life and showed me that you can be anything you want to be as long as you have a dream and a passion. What started as a demotion for me, turned into a lemonade-out-of-lemons success story. And now, more than 30 books later, I am lucky enough to be able to make my career doing something I absolutely love. So yeah, dreams really can come true.

   With that, I now present to you the life and times of someone I was very proud to call my friend and mentor, Herb Brooks.

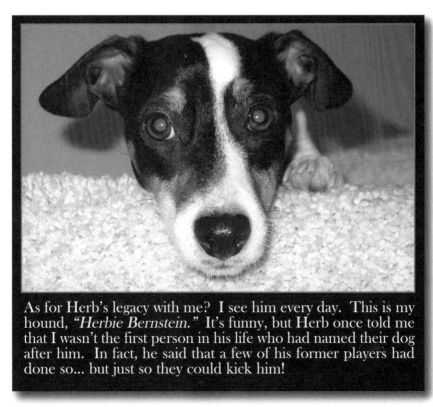

As for Herb's legacy with me? I see him every day. This is my hound, *"Herbie Bernstein."* It's funny, but Herb once told me that I wasn't the first person in his life who had named their dog after him. In fact, he said that a few of his former players had done so... but just so they could kick him!

CH. 1) NEVER FORGET YOUR ROOTS

One of the common denominators you will read about over and over in this book is how Herb Brooks never forgot his roots. He was extremely proud of where he came from, the hard working neighborhoods of the east side of St. Paul, and wore that as a badge of honor. It would shape who he was and how he treated others both on and off the ice.

Amidst the backdrop of the rolling hills and blue collar factories of the colorful east side of St. Paul, Herb Brooks grew up like most young boys in his neighborhood, with a love and passion for the sport of hockey. He was born on August 5, 1937, in St. Paul, Minn., to Herbert and Pauline Brooks. His father, an Irishman, was an automobile insurance underwriter. His mother, a Swede, worked both as a proofreader for a local publishing house, as well as a lifeguard during the Summers at Lake Phalen.

The family owned one car and lived in a modest duplex at the corner of Payne and Ivy Streets, just off of Queen Avenue on St. Paul's east side. East siders, as they were affectionately known, had a special close-knit bond with one another and took care of their own. It was a hard working community shaped by the Italians and Irish and Swedes and Poles who settled it. They worked long hours, at places such as the Hamm's brewery and the Whirlpool factory; and they played hard, at the many eating and drinking establishments that dotted colorful Payne Avenue.

Herb's father was a well known semi-pro hockey player who played on various teams throughout the Twin Cities. In fact, Herb Sr. played sometimes as many as five nights per week. Occasionally, Herbie and his younger siblings, David and Gayle, would pack up and go watch him play with their mother. They loved hockey and embraced it as a part of their fabric of life. Herb Sr. was also a coach and even started one of the very first youth hockey associations in the state of Minnesota. He would later coach his sons, teaching them to play the game the right way, tough, and with respect. Pauline, meanwhile, was an outstanding athlete in her own right and was an accomplished figure skater.

Herbie was close with his parents. His father enjoyed politics and encouraged open debate in the household. He believed strongly in the

Herbie (R) and his brother Dave (L), Herb Sr. was the coach

values of an honest days work and tried to instill those values into his children. Herbie's mother, meanwhile, helped to shape the softer, gentler side of his personality.

As kids, the Summers were all about hanging out at Lake Phalen, where mom could usually be found patrolling the beach. During the Winters, however, Herbie spent much of his time playing hockey on the neighborhood rinks and ponds. He took up the game at the age of four and loved everything about it, especially the fact that it made his father proud. He and David shared bunk beds growing up and loved to talk hockey until all hours of the night.

Herbie was a very good student in school and enjoyed reading books. He was very independent and very focused. He enjoyed setting and achieving goals that he would make for himself, even at a very young age. He was also very responsible and learned the values of hard work early on. In fact, by the time he was a teenager, he was working during the Summer months so that he could have the things that he wanted, such as a new bike or hockey skates.

Herbie also learned to appreciate his east side roots as a young man. The closeness of the community and the work ethic that embodied its citizens were values he would carry with him for a lifetime. Hockey, however, would be the glue that would bind them all together. Because of his passion for the game, he would remain close with many of his childhood friends from the neighborhood over the ensuing six decades.

As a kid, Herbie loved to follow the Olympics. In fact, his neighborhood idols were Jim Sedin and Wendell Anderson, who both won silver medals at the 1952 and 1956 Olympic Winter Games, respectively. Anderson, of course, would later go on to serve as both the Governor of Minnesota as well as a U.S. Senator, during the 1970s.

1952 Twin City

An outstanding athlete, Herbie went on to play hockey and baseball at St. Paul Johnson High School from 1953-55. On the ice is where he really left his mark though, where, as a senior, he led the Governors to a 26-1-2 record en route to winning the 1955 state championship. Johnson was a powerhouse in those days and had an extremely successful program with a lot of history behind it. Every little boy who grows up playing hockey in Minnesota dreams of one day playing in the state tourney, and that experience was one that Herbie would certainly never forget.

"Growing up in St. Paul I was a typical youth hockey player that hung around the rink and just fell in love with the game," said Brooks. "I think I was just like any other kid in that when I had a chance to finally make my high school team, it was a big thrill. Then, to win the state championship was very gratifying because it represented the guys I grew up with in the neighborhood. It was a grass-roots type of thrill, and those things stay with you for the rest of your life."

When the state tournament began that March, Johnson was slated to play Roseau in the fourth and final quarterfinal game of the day. But, as the Govs were getting ready to take the ice, they realized that the third quarterfinal contest between Minneapolis South and Thief River Falls, was heading to overtime. So, they waited patiently in their locker room for a winner to be announced. They waited and waited. Eventually, with no end in sight, the officials decided to let Johnson and Roseau take the ice after the ninth overtime period. By then it was rapidly approaching midnight and they figured the two games could just rotate between periods until somebody eventually won.

Finally, at 1:50 of the 11th extra session, South's Jim Westby scored the game-winner to end the unbelievable marathon. It would go down in the record books as the longest game ever to be played in tourney history, and remains there more than a half century later. Incidentally, and almost completely overshadowed, was the fact that Ken Fanger's first period goal was all that Johnson needed to hang on for a 1-0 win over Roseau in their much less dramatic contest.

Then, in the semifinals, Herbie put his Johnson squad up 1-0 midway through the first, while Stu Anderson and Roger Wigen each tallied in the third to give the Governors a 3-1 win, and a ticket to the Finals. There, Johnson and their Mill City rivals from Southwest faced off for the title in front of a packed St. Paul Auditorium crowd. The hero of the game would prove to be none other than Herbie, who got the Governors on the board at 2:32 of the first period. His teammate, Stu Anderson, then tallied about seven minutes later, only to see Brooks score his second goal of the game just a minute and a half after that. It would prove to be the final nail in the coffin as Coach Rube Gustafson's Governors cruised to a 3-1 victory.

"Winning the state championship was great, but my most memorable moment is not from the title game but the game we had to follow," said Brooks of the 11-overtime quarterfinal thriller. "We had to wait and wait in the dressing room; we'd take our skates off, put them on, shuffle our feet, this and that. It was hard to wait, and it was after one o'clock in the morning when our game was finally over, but we won and then went on to win the championship. Winning the state championship, that represented your neighborhood. I would have to say that it was my biggest thrill ever."

The 1955 St. Paul Johnson High School State Champs

Front Row: Karl Dahlberg, Herb Brooks, Roger Wigens, Tom Wahman, Jack Holstrom, John Patton.
Second Row: R. Gustafson (Coach), Rodney Anderson, Chuck Rodgers, Ken Fanger, Bill McKechnie, Ryan Ostebo, Stu Anderson, Tony Hudalla (Student Manager).

CH. 2) FOLLOW YOUR HEART, AS WELL AS YOUR HEAD

Brooks would turn down a scholarship offer elsewhere and instead choose to walk-on at the University of Minnesota. Like most kids who grew up in the Land of 10,000 Lakes, he too dreamt of one day wearing the Maroon and Gold. He also knew that Minnesota was where he wanted to live after he graduated, so it only made sense for him to lay down the foundation for his future right then and there.

With his clutch performance in the state tourney, Herbie had definitely proven that he was capable of playing at the next level. Before long the colleges were calling and he found himself with a few options to ponder.

"I had an interview with the Air Force Academy, because I really wanted to be a fighter pilot," said Brooks. "Unfortunately, because I was slightly color blind, I washed out of the Academy. I also had a scholarship at the University of Michigan, but my dad encouraged me to walk-on at the University of Minnesota and try to play for John Mariucci instead. So that was the route I took."

His dad asked him where he wanted to live when he was finished with school. He reminded him of his connections to the east side of St. Paul and of the job opportunities he would garner while staying closer to home. Herbie agreed. He knew that if he worked hard and played well that he would earn a scholarship in no time, and that is precisely how it would all play out.

Brooks came to Gold Country in the Fall of 1955 and wasted little time in making a name for himself. With his quiet demeanor and blinding speed, it didn't take long for him to get noticed.

"He was one of the fastest, if not *the* fastest, player in college hockey in that era," Mariucci would later recall.

Brooks and Mariucci didn't necessarily hit it off from the start, but he grew to respect and admire the fiery coach.

"At first I was scared to death of him," said Brooks. "I was fresh

out of high school. I remember in practices my first year he used to call me Pete. For the longest time he never knew my name, and I was terrified of him."

Over time, Brooks would learn a great deal from the man known throughout the Land of 10,000 Lakes as the *"Godfather of Minnesota Hockey."* In fact, he would later say that he had more to do with shaping his ideas in hockey than any other individual.

"I patterned several aspects of my coaching after John," said Brooks. " He was a pioneer and faced immense competition as a coach. When the 1980 Olympic team won the gold, John said it was one more piece to the puzzle for American hockey. I shared these hopes, dreams and aspirations with him, and was proud of the fact that there were 12 of us from Minnesota on that team.

"He was like a father to me, we were very close. He wasn't long on words, and didn't want to be everybody's buddy like some coaches try to be. John was an entirely different guy as a coach. You took care of yourself under him. He never called you to take care of you, or told you to go to class. His psychology of coaching was for you to take care of yourself, or get the hell out. You grew up pretty fast under him. He was a throwback, and was an entirely different coach than you'd see today. He was such a great guy. I remember the day they renamed Williams Arena in his honor. It was his happiest day, and such a memorable moment for him."

Herbie also knew that if Mariucci's legacy was going to be carried forward, it would require people like himself to work hard to grow the game and to make sacrifices every step of the way. It would require a lot of "leadership by example," and that was what Herb Brooks was all about.

"In all social causes to better an institution, there's always got to be a rallying force, a catalyst, a glue, and a magnet, and that's what John was for American hockey," Brooks said. "The rest of us just filled in after him."

Herbie had a great time as a Gopher and made many lifelong friendships at the University of Minnesota. His time on campus was a wonderful mix of athletics and academics, where he proved to be not only a good student in the classroom, but also on the bench. He listened and watched Coach Mariucci very intently, recording many mental notes and observations along the way. When it was all said and done, Brooks had scored a total of 33 points over his three-year career in Gold Country. Looking back, Brooks was grateful for the opportunity, but realistic about his options.

"There weren't many options for an American kid or a Minnesota kid in college hockey back then," recalled Brooks of his playing days on campus. "It was really tough. I always thought it was the toughest time of any Gopher era because of the Canadian kids who were coming down, the competition, and lack of NCAA rules in those days. It was really tough. Luckily, John (Mariucci) kept the door open for us. So it was very important to play for the U of M. It's not like it is today where there are a lot more hockey schools, and American kids have more opportunities. Playing for the Gophers then, when there were few opportunities, was real special. It was a real honor and it meant a lot."

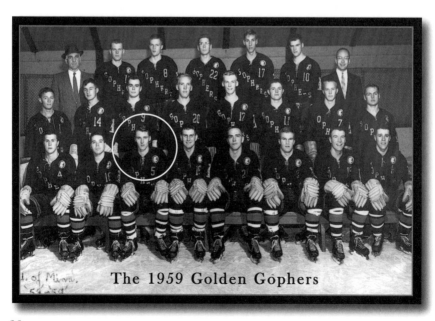

The 1959 Golden Gophers

Herbie could have also played baseball for the Gophers, but opted for hockey instead. Here he is as a member of the 1957 3M City League All-Stars.

CH. 3) DEFINE AND REDEFINE YOUR DREAMS

Herbie's dream was always about playing on an Olympic team. When that didn't happen, however, it forced him to redefine who he was and what he was made of. In the end, the experience would ultimately make him stronger and more resolute in his convictions.

With only a few months to go before graduation, Brooks decided to pursue one of his lifelong dreams, to play in the Olympics. He had always had a real romance with the Olympics and was thrilled to get the chance to represent his country at the upcoming 1960 Winter Games in Squaw Valley, Calif. Herb Sr. was not so thrilled with the idea though, and told his son to buckle down and graduate instead. He figured he was a long shot to make the roster and like any loving, conservative father, he wanted his boy to finish what he had started and to become something, like a lawyer or an accountant.

Herbie had his own plan though and wasn't about to pass it up. You see, back in those days there were only six NHL franchises and very few professional opportunities for American college kids wanting to play at the next level. The Canadians not only dominated the rosters of pro hockey during that era, they also controlled the front offices as well. As a result, it was a long shot for American kids to make it. So, Herbie dreamed of playing in the Olympics instead, which was at the time, the pinnacle for 99% of American kids. Brooks would work like hell to make that team to not only make his country proud, but also to make his father proud.

With that, Herbie tried out and made the 1960 U.S. Olympic team. The speedy winger played well in the exhibition games, even scoring 10 points in 15 games. Then, on the day before the team was to board a flight for Squaw Valley, Head Coach Jack Riley called him to tell

him that he was going to be the last player cut from the roster. Herbie was shocked. Coach Riley explained to him that after months of recruitment, he had finally been able to convince 1956 Olympic standout Bill Cleary to rejoin the team.

Cleary, who had earned All-American honors at Harvard, said he would come under one condition — that his brother, Bob, be able to play with him. Riley reluctantly agreed. So, in order to make room on the roster, he had to make one final cut. Sadly, it was Herbie. Bob Cleary's head was even cut and pasted over Brooks' in the official team photo, which had been shot weeks earlier.

Brooks was devastated. He immediately called home to ask his dad for some fatherly advice.

"I called home and my dad told me, 'Thank the coaching staff, keep your mouth shut and come home,' and that's what I did," he said. Herbie then returned to Minnesota to finish his degree and get on with his life. A few weeks later Herb and his dad sat down together in the living room to watch the U.S. team play against Czechoslovakia in the Finals. The Americans had just upset the defending champions from the Soviet Union in the semifinals, 4-3, the night before, and were now poised to make history.

Herbie sat and watched as his buddies, some of whom he grew up with on the frozen ponds of St. Paul, were about to play for a gold medal. The game roared back and forth and was tied at four apiece heading into the third period. Then, behind the Cleary brothers, the Americans went on to score five unanswered third-period goals and win the game, 9-4. As the team celebrated at center ice in an amazing moment of glory, Herb's emotions were running wild. He was torn. On one hand he was genuinely happy for his old pals. But on the other hand, he was jealous as hell, because they were living out his dream. He

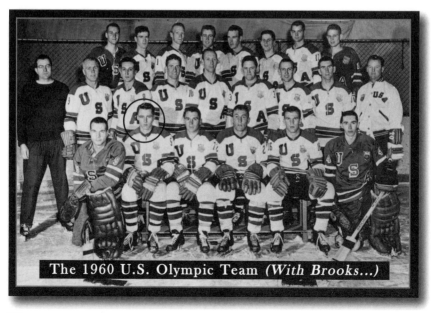

The 1960 U.S. Olympic Team *(With Brooks...)*

looked to his father for comfort.

At that very moment Herb Sr. looked back at his son, paused, and said: "Looks like Coach Riley cut the right guy...".

It was right then and there, on February 28, 1960, that Herbie knew his destiny. He was going to make the 1964 Olympic team, and one day, he was going to coach an Olympic team. Period. It was a defining moment that would change his life forever. It was a cruel and cold comment to be sure. But it would not define him. He would remember that line for the rest of his life though, and use it not to feel pity or to prove his old man wrong, but to drive himself towards success in everything he did.

Looking back, Herbie later realized that it just might have been the best motivational tool he could have ever gotten. His father had challenged his dreams and forced him to redefine who he was and what he was made of. In fact, it would shape his entire philosophy towards the game of hockey as well as his coaching ideologies for years to come. It was a tough lesson in humility, but one that would drive him towards perfection both on and off the ice.

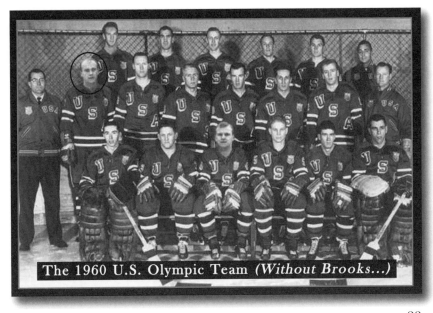

The 1960 U.S. Olympic Team *(Without Brooks...)*

CH. 4) SET GOALS IN LIFE AND THEN WORK HARD TO ACHIEVE THEM

Brooks was determined to make the most of a bad situation and he did just that. In fact, he would go on to play on a total of eight U.S. National and Olympic teams from 1960-70, more than any other player in American history. And, he had set a long term goal, to one day coach an Olympic team. In order to achieve that goal, however, he knew that he would need a lot of experience as both an international player as well as a coach. It would require a lot of hard work and literally years of patience. His long and arduous journey was about to begin.

The next chapter of Herbie's life was all about becoming a student of the game. He now had a goal; a long-term vision, and he was determined to achieve it. He was going to learn the international style of hockey first hand, as a player, and later apply that knowledge towards becoming a coach one day. First, however, he had to finish school, which he did that next semester. He would graduate from the University with a minor in Economics and a B.A. in Psychology — a degree he would put to use in more ways than one over the ensuing decades to come.

After spending the next six months serving in the Army at Ft. Leonard Wood, MO, Brooks returned to St. Paul and began working in the insurance business. He was also committed to keep training in order to make the next U.S. National team, which played in between the Olympic years. So, to keep in shape, he played off and on with some local semi-pro teams, including the St. Paul Steers and Rochester Mustangs. His plan worked. He made the 1961 U.S. National team and then earned a roster spot on the 1962 team that next year as well. His big break came the following year when, after training hard, he was named to the 1964 U.S. Olympic team. His dream of being an Olympic athlete was about to come true. And, to make it even sweeter, he would be joined out on the ice by his kid brother, David, who had also starred for the Gophers from 1961-63.

Traveling across Europe in preparation for the Winter Games in Innsbruck, Austria, proved to be a very valuable learning experience for

Herbie. He soaked things up like a sponge, analyzing how other teams played and prepared. He also paid close attention to the coaches, learning as much as he could from the way they conducted themselves both on and off the ice. The Americans finished a disappointing fifth at the tournament with an overall record of 3-5, but it was a marvelous experience for Brooks and it made him hunger for more.

Back at home that Summer, Herbie met a girl, only this time it was serious. Her name was Patti. She was a nurse at Devine Redeemer Hospital in South St. Paul, and they met late one night when he came in with a broken arm that he had suffered during a hockey game. She was from Yankton, South Dakota, and wasn't a hockey fan to say the least, but they started dating shortly after that and soon fell in love.

Meanwhile, Brooks had been named as the captain of the 1965 U.S. National Team. One of his teammates on that squad was Tim Taylor, who would go on to become the longtime head coach at Yale University and later coach the 1994 U.S. Olympic team.

"I have great memories of Herb from that time with him," recalled Taylor," He was the picture of grace when he played, a marvelous skater with tremendous body rhythm. He could play forward and defense and was a hugely effective player because he was so together out there. I remember the challenges in 1965 when we played the Russians, a real David-and-Goliath match up. Herb, as captain, went around the locker room telling us it was fun to play the Russians. He told us to enjoy the moment. He knew we were a little too in awe of the Russians. We knew how good they were."

From there, Herbie settled down. He and Patti were married that Fall and bought their first home on Hazelwood Avenue on the east side of St. Paul, not far from Harding High School. Ironically, the house had previously been owned by "Moose" Goheen, who was the first play-

Herbie & his brother Dave on the 1964 Olympic team

er from Minnesota ever to be inducted into the Hockey Hall of Fame in Toronto. Patti continued to work at the hospital, while Herbie sold insurance with the W.A. Lang Company. He also continued to compete as a member of the U.S. National team in preparation for the 1968 Winter Olympics.

The family then went from two to three in the Spring of 1967, when their son Dan was born. Shortly thereafter they moved to the St. Paul suburb of Mahtomedi, where they wound up living next door to Warren Strelow, one of Herbie's old neighborhood hockey buddies from St. Paul. The two were inseparable. Strelow would later serve as Herbie's longtime goalie coach with the University of Minnesota, the 1980 Olympic team, and later in the National Hockey League.

For Warren, it was just like old times back on the east side.

"Herbie and I lived by each other as kids and would play hockey together every night until they shut the lights out on us," recalled Strelow. "Then, we would sneak back and turn the lights back on and play for a few more hours. Sometimes the park cops would come down but they would let us play, they were great. Then, years later, every Sunday night we would go over to that outdoor rink to play. I had the key to the warming house and we would all go over there and play a pick-up game. Some of the old guys who played on Olympic teams would even join us and we would scrimmage against the high school kids. Herbie just loved that more than anything."

After playing on the 1967 U.S. National team, Herbie was named as the captain of the 1968 U.S. Olympic team which would compete in Grenoble, France. He was excited about the opportunity to once again represent his country. Despite his team finishing a disappointing sixth, as the Soviets continued their dominance over the world of hockey by winning their second gold medal in a row, he remained positive.

"The Olympics were always my goal," he said. "Playing in them was really a big thrill, and all things considered, it was one of the biggest highlights of my career."

With that, Herbie returned home and once again set his sites on preparing for the 1972 Winter Olympics, in Sapporo, Japan. He took off that next year to work, but then came back strong as a member of the 1970 U.S. National team. He had had enough after that, however, and ultimately decided to retire following that overseas campaign. He had paid his dues and was ready for his next challenge in life.

"I was playing, raising a family and trying to sell insurance," Brooks recalled. "My boss took me aside and said he thought I was biting off more than I could chew. He said that even if I made the team, I'd just be repeating myself."

Incredibly, he had spent nearly the entire decade playing for a total of eight U.S. Olympic or U.S. National teams — more than any player in the history of United States hockey. The sturdy winger-turned-defenseman had certainly paid his dues as a player by this point and was ready to parlay his decade of hockey knowledge into a coaching career.

Herbie & Lou Nanne
on the 1968 Olympic team

CH. 5) PAY YOUR DUES
AND EVENTUALLY YOU
WILL BE REWARDED

Brooks' hard work over the past decade would be rewarded with a couple of minor coaching positions, first with a Junior A team, and then as the freshman coach back at the University of Minnesota. He knew that if he could achieve success there, then bigger and better opportunities would surely follow. He had studied the game intensely during that time overseas and was anxious to apply that knowledge in formulating his own coaching style.

With plenty of practical experience under his belt, Brooks was eager to begin the next phase of his life as a teacher and mentor. Prior to the Olympics, he had learned the game under the tutelage of Rube Gustafson, at St. Paul Johnson, followed by John Mariucci, at the University of Minnesota. And, while he had learned a great deal from the American coaching staffs over the past 10 years as a player on various U.S. Olympic and National teams, he learned the most while simply observing his overseas opponents. He studied their tactics every chance he could and immersed himself into their cultures during overseas tournaments. He was fascinated by the Eastern Europeans, the Scandinavians and especially the Soviets. In fact, his own coaching style would be an amalgam of all three, combined with the toughness of the North American game as well.

After coaching at the youth bantam level, Brooks got his first gig back with his alma mater at the University of Minnesota, where he served as Coach Glen Sonmor's freshman coach. Glen was himself a former player who grew up learning the game in Canada. Herbie had played for Sonmor when he was an assistant with the Gophers under John Mariucci, and the two hit it off right away. Herbie would learn a great deal from Sonmor and apply those lessons to his own coaching philosophy over the ensuing years.

One of the things they had in common was that they both really liked tough kids who were not afraid to drop the gloves and mix it up. Glen, like Mariucci, was one tough S.O.B., and had been in his share of scraps over the years in pro hockey. Herbie would learn a great deal from those two about the importance of having tough, role players on your team in order to protect your skill players and to prevent the opposition from intimidating them.

In addition to working on the Gopher staff, Brooks also served

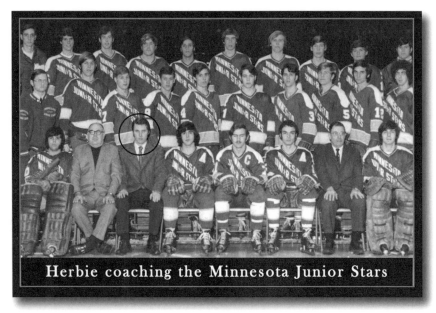

Herbie coaching the Minnesota Junior Stars

as the head coach of the upstart Minnesota Junior Stars of the Minnesota-Thunder Bay Junior A League. The circuit was for kids just out of high school who were on the bubble with regards to being able to play at the collegiate level. While many were talented skaters, others were just downright brawlers. It was a mix of the good, the bad and the ugly.

Brooks was notorious for spending long hours at the rink in those days, whether he was coaching or scouting or just talking hockey with reporters or coaches. He figured that as long as he was there, he was going to get as much accomplished as possible. He was a firm believer in multi-tasking and tried to be very efficient in every aspect of his life. In fact, he often carried that "kill two birds with one stone" mentality a step further after games, when he would park his car as seemingly far away from the front door of the arena as possible in order to get in a little extra exercise. That was Herbie.

In 1971 Brooks led his Junior Stars squad to a second place finish in the league standings. He saw the value of the junior program and knew that it was the perfect go-between for kids who needed a bit more seasoning before making the jump to the college level.

"That season, I had my own organization for the first time," remembered Brooks. "I worked with some excellent people, Ron Woodey, Harry Sundberg, Charley Hallman and Bob Sommers — guys who had the foresight to see Junior hockey as a way of helping the grow-

ing hockey program in the state."

It is interesting to note that during that off-season, Brooks was considered for the head coaching position at the University of Wisconsin, a job which ultimately went to fellow Gopher teammate and arch-rival, Bob Johnson. Scary to think that if that had happened it might have been "Badger-Herbie" instead of "Badger Bob."

In August Brooks got into his first spat with the Gopher Athletic Department. It would be the first of many. Herb was upset with the Athletics Director, Marsh Ryman, for not being allowed to travel with the varsity to the NCAA tournament. So, he resigned as the freshman coach out of principle. That next season, however, Sonmor resigned to take over as the head coach of the St. Paul Saints of the upstart World Hockey Association. Former Gopher Ken Yackel was named as the interim coach for the remainder of the season, but before long, Mariucci and Sonmor were lobbying for Herbie to catch a break. Newly appointed Athletics Director Paul Giel would wholeheartedly agree.

Sure enough, Brooks caught that break on Feb. 21, 1972, when he was named as the new head coach of the Gophers. At just 34, he would be the youngest coach in the Western Collegiate Hockey Association. He would also be inheriting a team which had just finished in the conference cellar. The underdog scenario was perfect for Brooks though, who vowed to give Minnesota "the most desirable hockey program in the country." It was a new challenge for him, and he dove in

Herbie with John Mariucci

head first, ready to take on the world.

One of the first people Brooks confided in was his old coach, John Mariucci, who couldn't have been prouder for his former pupil.

"John told me that it was important for me to keep giving opportunities to not only American kids, but especially to Minnesota kids," said Brooks. "He knew that like the professional ranks, the college ranks were filled mostly with Canadian players. It wasn't that John was anti-Canadian, he was just pro-American. He felt that our kids needed a chance to showcase their talents and it was up to us to give that to them. I completely agreed."

Brooks immediately started recruiting kids out of his Junior A league. He knew that those kids had a lot more seasoning than the kids who came right out of high school and they were tough. He knew that if he was going to be competitive in the rugged WCHA, he needed kids with grit who weren't afraid to get dirty. That blue collar, lunch pail attitude would resonate with Brooks and his tough east side mentality of how things should be done. He wanted character guys, and there would be plenty to choose from down there. He would use the program almost like his own personal minor league, sending high school seniors there for more seasoning and then calling them up when he felt they were ready or when he needed them. It was brilliant.

With his extensive knowledge and experience in European and eastern bloc hockey, Herb became an advocate of the Russian style of

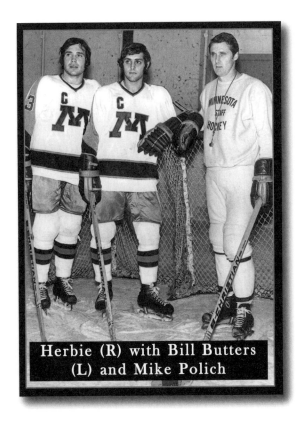

Herbie (R) with Bill Butters (L) and Mike Polich

play. In particular, he modeled much of his coaching style to that of the legendary Soviet coach, Anatoli Tarasov. He instilled many of the methodologies, training programs and systems that he had learned from the Russians into his own game plan. His teams would be known for their hustle, desire and work ethic — all reflections of Brooks' hard-driving motivational style of coaching.

ON COACHING & SALES...

"As far as my psychological and motivational style, I believe in setting high standards for players, being open and honest with them, and respecting an honest effort. I am always looking at an athlete and a team and addressing the psycho-physiological being.

"With regards to my own coaching style, I believe in setting high standards for my players. I never wanted to let them slide or have any sort of comfort zone. It is a combination of pushing or pulling them to those standards. I don't think good coaches put greatness into their athletes. You try to create an environment for athletes to pull this greatness out.

"I would also say that I am definitely not a book coach. In fact, I think there are too many book coaches today. You know it's like "time-out, I gotta run to the library..." . Instead, I would encourage those coaches to study and do research on the academic side of coaching. Then they could try to incorporate that research along with their personality to see how they can best sell those X's and O's to their players.

"Because really, when you are a coach you are just selling. You are selling team building, you are selling your systems of play, you are selling everything associated with making an individual better, and collectively your team better. I also think they have to be instinctive and be able to react on the turn of a dime, particularly under pressure. Coaching is really a battle for the hearts and minds of your athletes. It is as simple as that.

"I am also a big believer in the philosophy of 'it's not what you say, but how you say it.' I think having the ability to communicate and, once again, having the ability to sell your beliefs is the key to being a successful coach. You have to give your players something to believe in, then they will have something to belong to. Once they have something to belong to, then they have something to follow."

— *Herb Brooks*

CH. 6) MAKE THE MOST OF YOUR OPPORTUNITIES WHEN THEY PRESENT THEMSELVES

Brooks was finally in a position to take over a major college program, which in his eyes was ripe for change. It was the perfect opportunity for him to come in and implement his new European hybrid style of play. And, by virtue of the fact that his new team had just finished in the conference cellar, he had nowhere to go but up. There would be very little pressure on him to win right out of the gates either. It was an ideal situation for him and he was determined to make the most of it.

Brooks had a good nucleus of players for his first season behind the Gopher bench, 1971-72. His boys worked hard and would rebound from their disastrous 8-24-0 mark of the previous year to post a respectable 15-16-3 record. His Gophers ultimately finished the season by being swept in the WCHA Playoffs, however, by the University of Wisconsin, in Madison. It was a tough way to end the year, but Brooks had plenty to build on for his sophomore campaign.

Herbie was optimistic and knew that he had laid the foundation for a solid program. He knew that in order to keep getting the top Minnesota recruits, however, he was going to have to help promote the game of hockey throughout the state on a grass-roots basis. He was going to have to go out and build a feeder-program, a pipeline, to funnel the top kids towards the U of M.

So, with the help of Mariucci, he traveled from town to town, speaking at youth hockey functions and helping to set up new hockey associations in rural communities. It was "building the base of the pyramid," as Herbie used to say, getting more people involved from the bottom up. He was on a crusade; a mission, and luckily for us, that mission would change the face of hockey as we now know it.

Just when life couldn't have gotten any more hectic, the Brooks family grew again in 1972 when their daughter Kelly was born. For the first time in a long time, there was some stability in the Brooks household. Sure, there was traveling on the weekends during the season, but it wasn't as chaotic as when Herbie was globetrotting around the world as an international player. Life was manageable back on the home front and that allowed Herbie to become consumed with his team. He ate, drank and slept hockey, always pondering ways to better his team.

Brooks realized early on that in order for his teams to have a chance, they were going to have to be in shape... really good shape. In

fact, his practices were so tough that before long the players learned to love the weekends, when they had games, because they were like days off compared to his boot-camp practices. Players would skate until they puked and then they would skate some more. Fights broke out between players and oftentimes Herbie would let them go. "Go on, get it out of your system," he would say, "and then get the hell back to work."

"He'd say, 'You can cuss at me Monday through Thursday, but Friday you'll thank me,' "recalled All-American Mike Polich of Herbie. "He'd work the heck out of you. We'd wear these weighted lead vests, and we'd skate drill after drill. But you'd take 'em off on Thursday and feel like you could fly."

Nothing was off limits. Everybody had a role on Herbie's team and regardless of what that role was, in Herbie's eyes it was the most important role on the team. Herb was a master motivator and was able to convince each player; whether he was a goal scoring sniper, a mucker-grinder defenseman, a fourth line special teamer, or even a junk-yard brawler; that if he did not do his job, then collectively the team would fail. Nobody wanted that kind of pressure put on them, so they all worked their tails off. Brooks was committed to making each player feel account-able. He only wanted players who wanted to be there too, because loyalty went a long way with him.

"Herbie's practices? We used to say that if he did this to a dog, the humane society would throw him in jail," quipped former winger

Don Micheletti. "But it taught us to keep pushing each other as team-mates, and to be in shape for that third period so we could win. You know, Herbie originally offered me a half scholarship to play for him. I told him that Colorado College had offered me a full scholarship, but I was committed to the U of M. I told him that even though I needed the full ride, because my parents needed to save their money for my other family members who wanted to go to college, that I would still accept the half scholarship. Herbie looked at me, smiled, and said, 'I'm proud of you. I had a full scholarship waiting for you the entire time, but I want-ed to see how badly you wanted to be a Gopher.' "

The following season, Minnesota made history. After starting 0-4-1, the Gophers put together a nine-game winning streak and went on to lose only two of it's final 16 home games at Williams Arena. They fin-ished with a 14-9-5 record, good enough for second place in the WCHA behind Michigan Tech. They then went on to beat two tough Michigan and Denver teams in the WCHA playoffs, and suddenly found them-selves on their way to Boston, where they faced the top-ranked, home-town Terriers of Boston University in the NCAA Final-Four. The Cinderella Gophers felt right at home in the Boston Garden, as they pro-ceeded to knock off BU in a nail-biter, 5-4, thanks to Mike Polich's shorthanded goal at 19:47 of the third period to make it into the Finals. There, they faced their old WCHA nemesis, Michigan Tech, for the title.

The Gophers went back and forth with the Huskies throughout the first period, until John Sheridan scored late to give the Maroon and Gold a 1-0 lead. John Perpich then tallied to make it two-zip in the sec-ond. The Huskies came back though, scoring at 3:24 of the same peri-od, to get within one. It remained that way until the third period, when John Harris and then Pat Phippen both scored 12 minutes apart to put

Row 1 (L-R) – Equipment Manager Dick Brown, John Matschke, John Perpich, Eric Lookwood, Team Captain Brad Shelstad, Bill Moen, Cal Cossalter, John Harris, Manager Dennis Cossalter.
Row 2 (L-R) – Dr. V. George Nagobads (team doctor), Brad Marrow, John Sheridan, Bruce Carlson, Doug Falls, Dick Spannbauer, Mike Phippen, Robby Harris, Les Auge, Tim Carlson, Athletics Director Paul Giel, Head Coach Herb Brooks.
Row 3 (L-R) – Tom Vannelli, Warren Miller, Tom Dahlheim, Joe Micheletti, Bill "Buzz" Schneider, Mike Polich, Pat Phippen, Manager David Gurovitsch.

The 1974 NCAA Champion Gophers

the Gophers up for good. The Huskies added another goal with less than a minute to go, but it was too little, too late as the Gophers held on to win the game, 4-2. With that, Brooks' Gophers had their first ever NCAA hockey National Championship. Furthermore, it was the first time in more than a quarter century that a team comprised exclusively of Americans had won it all. For his efforts, Brooks was named as the WCHA Coach of the Year.

"It was tremendously gratifying getting the school's first championship coming from where we came from," Brooks would say. "The players weren't in awe of anything, and they were extremely strong mentally. Plus, they could really compete. They played well on the road, they played against the odds and overcame a lot that season. That first title was very special to me."

Brooks' former boss, Glen Sonmor, couldn't have been prouder. He knew all along that Brooks was going to be destined for greatness.

"Herbie just had that special quality about him which made him a winner," recalled Sonmor. "He was so intelligent too. He had an ability to see everything that was going on around him and then was able to pick out what was really important. Combine that with his unbelievable work ethic, and you knew he was going to be successful in whatever he did in life. That was Herbie. As a coach, he was such a great tactician. His players didn't love him, but they respected him and went to war for him. He was a no nonsense kind of a guy behind the bench and that was

all part of what made him a success. He didn't let anything slide either. I mean if something or somebody had to be confronted, then he would confront that situation right away and get it behind him. And what a great motivator he was. He could get his players to do things that they never imagined they were capable of doing, and that was just a marvelous quality. His honesty and forthrightness might have been his best qualities though. There was never any question as to where you stood with Herbie."

Brooks had instilled a new brand of pride and tradition into the program, starting with his newly designed jerseys which proudly featured the big Minnesota "M" on the front. The fans ate it up. When Brook arrived on the scene there were just a few thousand fans attending games at Williams Arena, now Gopher Hockey was one of the toughest tickets in town. Brooks promised he would bring, "exciting, dynamic people into the program," and he made it happen. More importantly, he stayed true to his word and did it all with Minnesota kids. Before long the chants of "Her-bee!, Her-bee!" echoed throughout the "Old Barn," giving the Gophers an amazing home-ice advantage that they had never known before. Brooks even had the team's bench area remodeled, adding a second players bench directly behind the original so that he would have the necessary space to pace behind his players — both figuratively and literally.

Ever the psychologist, Brooks knew which buttons to push on which people in order to get the most out of them. In fact, many felt it might have been his best quality as a coach. He loved to use certain players to make a point, but he had to be selective in who he singled out for his tirades, or it could backfire. He never wanted to humiliate a player, he only wanted to ride them hard so that they could reach their full potential. With Herbie, if he was riding a certain player, then that meant he cared about that player and was just demanding even more from him.

"Herbie really liked the players who worked hard for him," said

ON PRACTICING...

"I believe my practices were demanding and hopefully challenging. I tried to make our practices almost atypical situations so that games were easier — easier to adjust to the play, easier to read plays, easier to function on the ice. I was always striving to bring them out of their psycho-physiological comfort zones so that they were always improving their quickness, their execution of plays and the sharpness of their minds. I just always felt that the pace and the ability to execute at a high tempo was crucial. That way we were prepared for any set of circumstances that might have been thrown at us. I was always trying to lift the floor of their comfort zones during practice all the time." — *Herb Brooks*

Mike Polich. "I worked hard for him, and I think that is why we were close even after hockey. That work ethic that he instilled in me, drives me to this day in my own life and in my career. If you work hard, if you prepare and you are humble, then you will have success. What you put into it is what you are going to get out of it. If you work hard then you will have great dividends. It is up to you, and Herbie impacted me greatly on that. He just had a great work ethic. You know, Herbie hated prima donnas — guys with lots of talent but never used it. He would much rather have a bunch of guys with less talent but worked hard."

"I remember one time between periods during a game. Herb singled me out in front of the everybody and said 'Polich, you're supposed to be a leader on this team! You're the most selfish player and biggest prima donna out there!' Well, the younger players' eyes were wide open at that point and they were just in shock. Then, he leaves and slams the door behind him. So, just before the period starts he comes back in and as the players are filing out to hit the ice, he comes over to me and puts his arm around me. 'Now, Michael,' he says softly, 'show these guys how to play the game.' That was Herbie, he would break you down and then build you right back up to make his point."

Brooks also had a real gift with regards to judging talent and being able to assemble the right line combinations. He understood team chemistry and was really good at putting players together who could compliment each others talents as well as shortcomings.

"I remember one time I asked Herbie why in the world he would put Donnie Micheletti alongside Steve Christoff and Timmy Harrer on the same line," recalled former high school coach and longtime friend Larry Hendrickson. "He had these two gifted scorers in Christoff and Harrer, and then he was putting Micheletti in there, who was not a goal-scorer whatsoever. Herbie would tell me, 'that is the right line.' He just believed in it, and knew that they would all make each other better. Well, it worked. I mean by the time Mick (Micheletti) was a senior he was scoring a bunch, and it turned out to be the perfect balance to that line. Mick kept them in line and protected them in front of the net. He just made the other guys better. As a result, his skill level went up, he got better and the team got better."

"Herbie just had that gift to be able to identify talent and to put the right combinations of guys together out there to work as a team. You know, even though Christoff and Harrer were both outstanding players, Herbie let them know that they weren't very good without Mick. He reminded them that he did things that they couldn't do, and that they needed him. Herbie celebrated players' differences and used that to make his teams better. He didn't need 20 'Mr. Hockey's' that were all goal scorers, he knew that he needed a blend of talent to be successful and that is what he did. It was a team game for Herbie and he reminded his players that every one had a role on the team and that they won and lost as a group. Period."

Minnesota had a great season in 1974-75, finishing first in the WCHA, and advancing all the way back to the NCAA Final Four in St. Louis. There, behind Warren Miller's hat trick, the Gophers beat Harvard, 6-4, to return to the Finals. Rival Michigan Tech was able to exact a little revenge though as they upset the defending champs from Minnesota, 6-1, to claim the crown.

That off-season, Herbie began to enjoy the fruits of his labor a little bit when he moved his family to a beautiful home on Turtle Lake. The kids were in school by this point and his wife Patti had decided to go back to work as a part-time nurse at St. Joseph's Hospital in St. Paul. Life was good.

Back on the ice, Herbie's Gophers rallied back in 1975-76 to win their second straight WCHA title with a 24-8-0 mark. The team had

ON TEAM BUILDING...

"It's up to the coach to create an environment which has a high level of comradeship, at all times reinforcing team concepts stressing strength of association and the power that can be attained when working together. The team reflects your value system, your instincts, your philosophies, and it is just a matter of how well you can articulate it and sell it to your players." — *Herb Brooks* gone through a pretty rough stretch during the regular season though, and Brooks needed to take some drastic measures to get his boys back on track. He had learned a lot over the past few seasons behind the bench and had a few tricks up his sleeve. One of them was simply to recognize when to back off and chill out a little bit. That wasn't an easy thing for a control freak like Herbie to do, but it proved to be an extremely effective motivational tool.

"I remember getting swept up at Michigan Tech," recalled former Gopher defenseman Reed Larson. "Herb was so upset that instead of flying home he made us take an all-night bus trip back to Minneapolis. I can still remember stopping in the middle of Wisconsin to take a leak on the side of the road because the beer was about three inches deep on the floor of the bus. Then, we were out in the snow banks having a snowball fight, shoving each other into the deep ditches. That was just a hilarious time, but something I will never forget. Herbie would punish us by making us bus home, but then reward us with beer, knowing that what we probably needed was to let our hair down a little bit. Well, we went on to win the national championship that year."

The Gophers biggest rival during this era was Wisconsin. There was a lot of bad blood between the two teams and Herbie used to do whatever he could to stir it up and make things a little more interesting. One time before a big series in Madison, Herbie even accused the Wisconsin fans of being a bunch of drunks. He and Badger Coach Bob Johnson didn't get along either, which only added fuel to the fire. There were a lot of brawls back in those days between the players and the fans used to pack the house to see it up close and personal. One time Herbie even got into the fray when a drunk Badger fan got up in his face and started screaming at him. Herbie reacted by throwing the guy into a wall, which resulted in the Police arresting the fiery coach on the spot. Brooks was tough and he expected his players to be tough as well.

The Gophers opened the post-season that year by playing a classic against Michigan State in East Lansing. In that game the Gophers

ON MOTIVATION...

"Motivation is really a combination of things. Obviously communication is very important. It is the ability to sell a concept. Sometimes it's the all important four words: 'ask questions and listen.' Coaching is selling. You're just selling Xs and O's and you're selling team building. So, to be a good coach you have to be a good salesman. You have to get your players to somehow buy into your system and your philosophies. That is the key. Players must know that you care about them. I am not a touchy-feely type of a person but I try to show my respect and caring for them in other ways."

— *Herb Brooks*

downed the Spartans, 7-6, in triple overtime behind goalie Jeff Tscherne's NCAA record 72 saves. From there, they advanced back to the NCAA Tournament in Denver, where they downed Boston University, 4-2, in the semifinals. Next up was a rematch with Michigan Tech for all the marbles. Down 3-0 early, the Gophers rallied behind goals from Tom Vannelli, Joe Micheletti, Bill Baker, Tom Gorence, Pat Phippen and Warren Miller, to beat the Cats, 6-4, and win their second NCAA championship in three years.

Most of Brooks' top players off of that team either graduated or turned pro after that, forcing the coach to begin a difficult rebuilding process. For those who graduated, Brooks was grateful for their service. And, for those who chose to leave school early to play professional hockey, that was fine too. It was going to be a tough road to hoe without his top players, but Herbie was up to the challenge.

"I'm never going to discourage a player from turning professional if the money is right," Brooks would say.

He took it as a compliment if a kid was good enough to come through his program and then be considered talented enough to play at the next level in the NHL. The bottom line was that Herbie was just going to have to work harder to stay on top. He knew that he had to become a better recruiter and salesman in order to keep achieving that level of success. He needed to raise the bar, his bar, and that is exactly what he did.

The constant traveling wore on Brooks, but it was all a part of what he did and who he was. Traveling had always been a part of the equation, first as a player, and then as a coach. And, if he wasn't on the road for a game, he was oftentimes on the road scouting kids from Roseau to Rochester, which could be extremely time consuming. It got to be a grind, but he managed to keep it all in perspective.

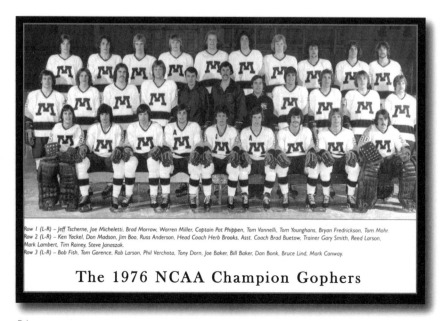

Row 1 (L-R) – Jeff Tscherne, Joe Micheletti, Brad Morrow, Warren Miller, Captain Pat Phippen, Tom Vannelli, Tom Younghans, Bryan Fredrickson, Tom Mohr.
Row 2 (L-R) – Ken Yackel, Don Madson, Jim Boo, Russ Anderson, Head Coach Herb Brooks, Asst. Coach Brad Buetow, Trainer Gary Smith, Reed Larson, Mark Lambert, Tim Rainey, Steve Janaszak.
Row 3 (L-R) – Bob Fish, Tom Gorence, Rob Larson, Phil Verchota, Tony Dorn, Joe Baker, Bill Baker, Dan Bonk, Bruce Lind, Mark Conway.

The 1976 NCAA Champion Gophers

"I know that it was difficult at times for Patti, with me being gone on the road so much," said Herbie. "But that was how things were in our lives and we had just gotten used to it over the years. We tried to make the best of it though and enjoy the time that we did have together. I remember one time she accused me of loving hockey more than her. I said 'Yeah, but I love you more than golf and hunting...'. She got a kick out of that one."

The 1977 and 1978 seasons were rebuilding years for the Gophers as the team wound up with seventh and fourth place finishes, respectively. There were some ups and downs during that time, but through it all Herbie managed to stay positive. Believe it or not, he was even able to keep his sense of humor. One of his favorite players was Jim Boo, a tough S.O.B. whose role on the team was crystal clear: to beat the crap out of anybody who messed with his team's top players. Herbie loved role players like that and made them feel like their role was just as important as that of his top All-American. Boo was a character and recalled a couple of funny instances during this rough stretch.

"I remember one night we were playing in Denver and my father made the trip out to see me," recalled Boo. "We lost, and afterward I snuck out of the hotel to see my dad for a few beers. Well, wouldn't you know it, but as I am sitting there with my dad having a cold one, the wait-ress comes over and says someone from across the bar bought me a beer. Thinking it might be a pretty lady, I turned to look. Only who do I see toasting me? Herbie. I knew right there that I was in big trouble. So, he comes over and says 'Jimmy, you might as well enjoy this one because you are going to pay for it tomorrow...'. Well, when we got home that next day we all went right to the rink from the airport and put on our wet equipment and skated. I remember just dying out there doing laps and he skates up to me and says, 'How's that beer tasting now Jimmy?'."

"Then, there was another funny incident which took place up in North Dakota," he added. "You know, I was never known for being a goal-scorer, but I will never forget my first one. It came after I miscalcu-lated a clearing pass in front of our own net and I actually scored on my own goalie. I felt terrible, and out of frustration I hacked the guy out front who was poke-checking me. The ref gave me a quick penalty and to add insult to injury, I got hit in the head with a dead fish on the way to the penalty box. Well, after I got out of the box — which was the safest place to be at the time, as far away from Herbie as possible, Herbie says, 'Congratulations Jimmy, you finally got one!'."

That off-season Brooks got his first taste of international coaching experience when he guided the U.S. National team at the World Games in Moscow. It was a great opportunity to test his skills against the world's best, and it gave him an chance to observe the wide open international style of hockey again — something he had been craving.

"Personally, it gave me a thrill to see how great the international game has become" said Brooks. "The Russians, Swedes, Czechs and Finns have a tremendously exciting brand of hockey."

In 1979 Brooks' Gophers made it back to the promised land yet again. Brooks had recruited a solid group of freshman and sophomores that season and they would step up when called upon. The team went through its share of ups and downs that season but finished the year ranked as the No. 1 team in the country. At one point, however, the team was going through a rough stretch. So, Herbie pulled out one of his old tricks from up his sleeve in an effort to build some team chemistry. It was unorthodox, but effective.

"I'll never forget during my junior year with the Gophers, 1979, we were in a slump and had lost like six straight games in a row," recalled Robb McClanahan. "It was a really tough stretch and we were just down. So, I remember we were in Denver, and we had just lost. Herbie then brought everybody back to the hotel and said that nobody could go out that night and that everybody had to stay in. Then, he led us to a conference room at the hotel that he had gotten, and in there was beer and beer and beer and beer. I can't even remember if there was pizza in there or not, but we stayed in there all night and drank like fish. We just had a great time and really blew off some steam. We talked, we let our hair down and we relaxed. That was hard for Herbie to do, but he knew when to do that kind of thing and when not to. Shortly thereafter we got it together and we went on to win the national championship that year. That was Herbie. When we were playing poorly he laid off of us a little bit, but when we were playing well that is when he really kicked our asses."

In the playoffs, Minnesota went on to sweep both Michigan Tech and then the University of Minnesota-Duluth, before knocking off Bowling Green to earn a trip back to the NCAA Final Four, which was at Detroit's Joe Louis Arena. There, behind Eric Strobel's hat trick, Minnesota held on to beat New Hampshire, 4-3, in the opener.

ON WINNERS...

"Winners in my opinion are those who are willing to make sacrifices for the unknown, both for themselves and for the team. Once you have that, then the results take care of themselves."

— *Herb Brooks*

It was now on to the Finals, where the Gophers would meet up with their neighbors from North Dakota. Minnesota jumped out to an early lead in this one on goals from Steve Christoff, John Meredith and team captain, Bill Baker, to make it 3-1 after the first period. The Sioux then rallied in the second, narrowing the gap to 3-2. Then, early in the final period, Neal Broten, the freshman sensation from Roseau, scored on a fabulous, sliding chip shot in what would prove to be the game winner. UND added another goal late, but the incredible goaltending of Gopher senior netminder Steve Janaszak proved to be the difference as the Gophers held on to win, 4-3, and claim their third NCAA National Championship in just seven seasons.

"We were playing against a tremendous North Dakota team," said Brooks. "I think they had 13 guys that turned pro that next year. Broten scored a dramatic goal, sliding on his stomach and hitting a chipshot over the goalie. It was incredible. I remember speaking at a Blue Line Club meeting the year before and saying that we were going to win it all that next season. It leaked out in the press and went across the country, putting a lot of pressure on our team. I kind of wish I wouldn't have said it now. But I just felt really strong about that team. I put a lot of pressure on those kids and I really raised the bar. But, because of their mental toughness and talent, we won the championship."

Brooks then got the call he had been waiting a lifetime for. After several interviews and much lobbying, he had been named as the head coach of the 1980 Olympic team which would compete at the Winter Games in Lake Placid, New York. He wasn't the USOC's first choice, but he would definitely turn out to be the right choice. For Herbie, it was truly a dream come true.

"Having played international hockey for so many years, it gives me an awfully warm feeling to be selected as head coach for the 1980

The 1979 National Champion Gophers

Olympics," said Brooks of his new job. "I'm extremely honored and humbled. To be picked when there are so many outstanding amateur hockey coaches in the nation, well, let's just say it's something I never really expected to happen."

With that, Brooks' longtime assistant coach and former player, Brad Buetow, was named as the interim head coach of the Gophers. In all, Brooks had achieved truly amazing heights during his tenure in Gold Country. From 1972-79, he won three NCAA National Championships; finished second once; and posted a career record of 175-100-20, for a .636 winning percentage. Brooks also guided five All-Americans and also sent 23 of his protégés on to play in the NHL. When it was all said and done, Brooks was able to reflect upon his success in Gold Country and how he had achieved it.

"We went to the Finals four of my seven years there, and we made a great run of it," he said. "I think I put a lot of pressure on the players, and I had a lot of expectations of them. I didn't give them an 'out,' and I think I was always able to find the kids who were really competitive. The common denominator of all the guys who played throughout my seven years was that they were really competitive, very hungry, very focused, and mentally tough — to go along with whatever talent they had. I think that really carried us."

Brooks was clear about his motivations, however, and was anxious to achieve the next goal that he had set for himself many years prior — to be in a position where he would be considered to serve as the head coach of a U.S. Olympic team. He always had a plan, even from day one, and he stayed true to it every step of the way.

"When I started coaching at the University of Minnesota I wanted to coach an NCAA championship team," he said. "And, I also wanted to coach an Olympic team. While at the University, I wanted to create a positive environment for our players so that they could grow as peo-

ON MOTIVATION & MENTAL TOUGHNESS...

"Motivation and mental toughness go hand in hand. Personally, I hate to lose. At one point in my career I was more scared of losing than wanting to win. I still hate to lose, but my perspective and outlook has changed. My aim now is all about now, today. Alcoholics Anonymous tells us to take it "one day at a time," and whether you are in that group or not, it makes sense to apply that philosophy to sports as well. I try to keep events in their proper perspective, this helps my strength, energy and enjoyment in life. What I am doing is then easy, it flows, it's natural, it's the difference between a standard transmission and an automatic. Then, and only then do I perform my best."
— *Herb Brooks*

ple, grow as athletes, and receive a good education. But the overriding motivation for me while at the University of Minnesota, was to coach an Olympic team. To do that, I knew that we had to be very successful in order to even be considered. The entire time I was there though, I was thinking about coaching the Olympic team. I am very proud of winning three NCAA national titles, but to go on to become the coach of Team USA was what it was all about for me."

ONE OF HERBIE'S
COMMENCEMENT SPEECHES...

"In the next few weeks, thousands of area high school seniors will place tasseled mortarboards on heads full of plans, dreams and schemes. How often do these plans work out? What effect does the great novelty of life beyond high school have on a graduate's hopes?

"I think back to a question Peppermint Pattie once asked Charlie Brown. 'Do you know any good rules for living?', to which Charlie answers: 'keep the ball low; don't leave your crayons in the sun; use dental floss every day; don't spill the shoe polish; always knock before entering; don't let the ants get in the sugar; and always get your first serve in.' Confused, Patti then wanted to know, 'Do they work? Will those rules give me the good life?' She isn't certain, even though what Charlie has told her is conventional wisdom, what everybody already knows.

"I am not so old as to have lost my memory of what must be surging through the minds of you who are about to step from the sheltered life of the student into active participation in the prime of your life. We all have anxieties, so what should we do? We should face them, head on. Let me ask you, have any of you ever been right up against the wall; and gone nowhere? What can you do? When every trick in the book has been tried; when every letter of the rule has been followed; is there anything else that can be done? Or is this it; is this the end? Is this wall the limit of possibility? Are we convinced that there is nothing more for us beyond this wall? Have we decided that there is no way through it?

"All of us have been up against such walls before. Life is full of walls: between youth and adulthood; between college and our life's work; between people — children and adults, husbands and wives, and friends. History is full of walls. Moses and the people of Israel ran right up against the wall, as did their father Jacob before them. They no sooner escaped to freedom from Egypt when they ran up against the wall of water in the Sea of Reeds. There they were, the sea in front of them, the Egyptians in horses and chariots behind them. The people of the United States of America escaped to freedom from the old world only to run up against the wall in the new world of the Mason-Dixon Line.

"Everyone must face such a wall, no one escapes. And finally, as for all of us, there lies ahead the wall of death. What is incredible about all this is that we know there is only one answer to the wall, and that is we must struggle to get through it. But most of us would rather do anything else than face that wall. And not one of us really wants to face it at all. Life should not be this way. The wall never should be there in the first place. How did the wall ever get there between husband and wife? What happened to the bright expectations that contrast so painfully with reality? How did the wall ever get there between parent and child? What happened to the dreams that were dreamed while bringing the child home from the hospital? What happened to the plans for raising the perfect child? What happened to the fun and joy anticipated at the beginning? And what happened to the dreams, plans and joy anticipated when first setting out on life's work?

"Something has gone wrong. We know that. We know something

is radically wrong. What a vast difference there is between the way life could be and the way it actually is. Yet that is the way life is, and has been from the beginning. And so the way lies ahead of us. We cannot force our partner to fit our dream of marriage, we cannot force our children to be what we want them to be any more than God could force us to stay in the garden. And so we work and struggle with the realities of life and the actualities of existence. That is our choice. Do we face the realities of life and struggle with the wall that stands before us, or do we turn away, refusing to go through the wall, refusing the struggle, refusing to face life as it really is? Of course it is easier to let things slide, to follow the path of least resistance. And yet there are two things we forget. If we decide to turn around again, the wall will still be there, bigger than ever. And if we do not face the wall, we may not see the trap door at our feet.

"How difficult it is to have faith enough to run forward against a doorless wall up to the last fraction of an inch in the certain hope it will surprise us and let us through. But we cannot possibly know the door will open if we do not go all the way. The minute we stop, the second we decide that it cannot possibly happen, then the door never opens and we never know what is on the other side.

"The 1980 U.S. Olympic hockey team ran head on into such a wall. But they refused to stop and instead made the decision to go right through it. It was not that they knew they would win; they could not possibly know that. But they faced the realities of life. They knew how good the Russians were. They knew how badly the Russians had already humiliated them just a few weeks earlier. Beat the Russians? Impossible. Or was it? They knew they were young and inexperienced, but they refused to take the easy way out. They skated head-on against the wall, never once halting and deciding there was no way through; never once telling themselves that they could not win. No stress, no pressure; just joy and happiness.

"And yet there is still one more reason. For we have to ask, why do we, or anyone, even start forward toward the wall at all. Because that is the way life begins. The will-to-live, the breath of life, the pull of possibility; we are the ones who decide whether to stop or keep going.

"But why the wall, why the struggle? So that our joy may be full. There is no other way, but we never know if we stop before we go through. So why struggle? And struggle: for what? Which is exactly what the Soviet team expected our team to think. But those kids had not made that decision. And neither should we. Or, we are going to lose out on such a great joy. That joy is peace of mind.

"No, you will probably not be as good as you want, or be able to achieve everything you would like if one word is a part of your vocabulary — 'IF.' IF I would have done this and IF I would have done that. IF has become America's disease, a mental cancer that has only one cure all: peace of mind. That is the intangible that will last and endure. And this value is more important than the game or events that occasion them. It is as simple as that. Our philosophy should be simple. Nobody should convince us that we have ever accomplished enough. "Congratulations and good luck."   — Herb Brooks

CH. 7) WHEN YOUR LONG TERM GOAL FINALLY COMES TO FRUITION, "PLAN YOUR WORK AND THEN WORK YOUR PLAN..."

Brooks' dream of one day being in a position to coach a U.S. Olympic team had finally come true. Now, he had the awesome responsibility of assembling a team worthy of winning a gold medal against the world's best. A detailed task-master, Brooks would leave no stone unturned in his quest to find the *right* players. For Brooks, it wasn't about the best players, it was about the *right* players.

Despite being just 42 years-old, Brooks had a lifetime of experience under his belt. He would now be called upon to do something that hadn't been done in two decades, however, win an Olympic hockey gold medal. Herbie was up for the task. He knew that there were other candidates with more experience and with more political clout who were in the running. But in the end, the selection committee decided to take a chance and give him a shot. They loved his enthusiasm, his work ethic and most of all, his passion. They wouldn't be disappointed.

"The Olympians, the amazing athletes like Jesse Owens, they are the ones who have always captivated me," said Brooks. "The Olympics are a world sporting spectacle on an international stage. It's national pride with so much wonderful history. I grew up with that history, so to me the Olympics transcend the game itself."

Brooks now had the enormous responsibility of selecting the players to fill out his roster. It was not going to be a dream team of all-stars either, no way. He didn't necessarily want the best players, he wanted the *right* players. He had a vision. He was going to incorporate a radical new style of play and he wanted a very specific type of player who was going to thrive in that type of system. Everybody would have a role on his team and no one individual was going to be any more or less important than anybody else. It was going to be all about the team, not about the individuals. Brooks reinforced the words "we and us," while staying away from "I and me."

He didn't want to take any chances, so he researched literally hundreds of qualified candidates, made countless phone calls, and tried to find out which players were the ones he could count on when it really mattered. He recruited winners, players who had won championships before at various levels of play and were used to winning. That was an extremely important criteria, he wanted guys who had tasted the fruits of success and would be hungry for more.

"When he had to pick the 1980 team, I remember Herbie calling the high schools of the potential Olympians to find out their records on grades; if they got into trouble; did drugs; and what kind of people they were," recalled Herb's brother Dave. "When I asked him why the hell he was doing that, he said that he wanted to know what kind of player he was going to have when it came down to the last two minutes of a game. He said he wanted to know which kids he should have on the ice come clutch time."

Finally, after months of research and due diligence, Brooks was ready to begin. He had assembled a diverse advisory panel of experts and encouraged input from all of them on a variety of issues. They had been in contact with nearly every Division I and II college coach in the nation, trying to solicit information and recommendations. Brooks personally flew cross-country dozens of times to see as many of the kids in person as possible. From there, a series of truly "open" try-outs were held to see if there were any diamonds in the rough which might have flown under the radar. A point system, that had been set up by Brooks, was implemented which assigned a numerical value for each individual players' strengths and weaknesses.

With that, the 68 players from across the country with the highest point totals were invited to the National Sports Festival in Colorado Springs that August for the opportunity to compete for one of just 26 roster spots. The players were all sent a dry-land training program to study in advance. Herbie was already testing them to see which ones would follow their instructions.

Once they all flew in, they were divided up into four teams. They would be tested and retested on everything from basic fundamental skills, to being timed by radar guns in order to measure their acceleration levels and top speeds. It would be a grueling two week training camp, but a necessary one. Brooks was committed to finding the *right* players for his team and would leave no stone unturned in the process.

One of the final tools Brooks utilized at the training camp was a massive psychological test which consisted of more than 300 questions he had specially prepared for the players. Brooks, who had earned a psychology degree in college, designed the test as a practical means of evaluating not only book smarts, but also street smarts. He wanted to know how certain players would react under various types of stress, and the test was going to show him that. Again, he was searching for a specific type of player and this was just another hoop the candidates would have to jump through in order to make the final cut.

While most of the players simply took the test without thinking twice, one player simply refused: Jim Craig. Craig, an All-American goaltender at Boston University, had played for Brooks on the 1979 U.S. National team at the World Championships. He knew that he belonged on the roster and didn't feel like he needed to take any psychological test to prove it.

"I am not taking your test," he would tell the coach.
"Really. Why's that?", asked Brooks.
"It's a bunch of B.S.", he would say.
"Well, you just took it," quipped the fiery coach, "you told me everything I needed to know."

That was Herbie, always pushing buttons and always keeping his players off guard. One thing was for sure, nobody was going to be guaranteed a spot on his team. They would have to earn it and prove to him that they deserved to be there. Brooks didn't care about politics or nepotism or anything else. He had a job to do and that was to select a group of individuals capable of learning a revolutionary new wide open style of hockey, so that they could win a gold medal. Period. For Brooks, it was personal.

Brooks wanted proven competitors who were not only tough and gritty, but who were young and had fresh legs. He also wanted smart, college educated kids who were extremely open minded about trying new things. He was tired of the traditional North American dump-and-chase style of hockey which had been the norm for so many years, and was about to introduce a radical new system. He wanted kids who he felt would be receptive to this as well as kids who he felt that he could mold into champions.

He wanted kids who had the self confidence to not be afraid to

break down old stereotypes and to be flexible. Brooks was on a mission to beat the Soviets and the Europeans at their own game of speed and finesse, and he needed his players to rethink everything from diet and exercise to on-ice strategy and tactical systems. Selfish, self-centered and ignorant players were going to be shown the door. He didn't care if they were good enough to go on to play in the NHL, he couldn't afford to have any cancers on his team who might infect the others. Again, the method to his team-building madness was all about choosing the *right* players, not the best players. There was a big difference.

"You have to start with a sound value system," Brooks would say, "and you can't buy values."

The Olympic, or international, style of hockey was a much different one than most Americans were used to. It features much more passing with far less physical play. The game is played on a much larger ice sheet too, with an extra 3,000 square feet of real estate. The kids he would select would have to be quick and they most certainly were going to have to be in the best physical shape of their lives. That was something he would personally make damn sure of.

To get the kids into this new mindset was going to be tough. Each and every one of the players before him had aspirations of playing in the National Hockey League. But, in order to do so, they had to impress the scouts and general managers who would need to feel confident in their abilities to play that type of rough, physical hockey; not the

wide open, pass-first, international one that Brooks was about to teach them. Everything was going to be different. The players would have to learn not to retaliate when agitated and provoked, something completely foreign to the typical North American player's psyche. Brooks' system was complex, but he was a great teacher. As he was fond of saying, "My problem has always been that when people ask me what time it is, I want to tell them how to build a watch."

Finally, after what probably seemed like an eternity of on and off the ice evaluations and observations, Brooks made the big announcement at a late-night session. The players all gathered around and Herbie spoke from his heart. For those who had made the team, he congratulated them and told them that they had better get ready to work harder than they had ever worked in their lives. For the others, who didn't make it, he wished them well in their future hockey or life endeavors.

He knew that for some it would be the beginning of their professional careers, and for others it would be the end of the line. He knew the feeling. He had been there before and reminded them that he wasn't upset about being the last player cut from the 1960 U.S. Olympic team. He told them it was painful, but that he knew that the coaches had made the right decision — because in the end they won the gold medal.

Brooks tried to be as honest and fair as he could and the players respected that. Take for instance the issue with Mark Johnson, who had been an All-American at the University of Wisconsin. It was widely known in hockey circles that there was some bad blood between Herbie and Mark's father, "Badger Bob," who was the head coach at UW. Sure, Brooks had issues with his dad, but he chose Mark to be a member of the team regardless. He knew that Mark was extremely talented and wasn't about to let his personal feelings get in the way of something like that. That was the kind of guy Herbie was.

Herb then took his 26 protégés aside for a few words of wisdom. He wanted to share a bit of advice from what he had learned as a member of two previous Olympic teams. He looked at them all standing there; wide-eyed and ready to take on the world. It was the youngest Olympic hockey team ever fielded with the average age being just 22.

ON CHARACTER...

"At elite levels of competition, coaches and managers are always looking for people with character, or what they call the 'intangibles.' What constitutes good character? I would say self managers who are motivated by challenges, are mentally tough and have good attitudes. All are important and complex, especially motivation and attitude. Those types of individuals, who are highly motivated and have a positive attitude, see possibilities in tough situations rather than obstacles."

— *Herb Brooks*

He then asked them to "sacrifice for the unknown; to be willing to lay it all on the line; and to be ready to take a leap of faith." The long, arduous seven month journey ahead had just begun.

With that, the new teammates went out and celebrated at a local bar. Nine of the players were former Gophers, and they knew what was in store for them down the road. They knew that they were going to be working harder than they had ever worked before. So, they relaxed, had some beers and enjoyed the moment. For the other players, who were mostly from the east coast, they had no idea what sort of grueling punishment was coming just over the horizon.

The team reassembled a short time later in the Twin Cities, where they would be headquartered. They would practice at the St. Paul Auditorium, now the Roy Wilkins Auditorium, and use the old St. Paul Saints' (WHA) locker room facilities. The players now had to learn a completely foreign style of hockey in less than 180 days. So, they hit the ice. Brooks wasted little time in getting them prepared; pushing, prodding and yelling at them throughout his marathon practice sessions. The players were shocked at just how hard he was driving them. He wanted them to be in the best physical shape of their lives for the long journey ahead. He expected them to have plenty of gas left in the tank come the third period of a big game, when their opponents would be dogging it.

His torture tool of choice? "Herbies." "Herbies" were Brooks' take on old fashioned wind sprints that could induce fear into even the strongest player. Players would line up at the end line, skate to the blue line and back; skate to red line and back; skate to far blue line and back; and then skate all the way down to the opposite end line and back. That was one "Herbie." After about 10 "Herbies," guys would either puke or wish they could puke. But Brooks knew that the Russians could do "Herbies" in their sleep. They were the best conditioned athletes in the

world in his eyes and were always hitting their stride deep into the third period. It had nothing to do with emotion or adrenaline, it had everything to do with the fact that they worked harder than everybody else and were willing to go that extra mile to be in world class condition. Brooks was determined to have his boys go that extra mile too.

Brooks' new offensive game-plan, called the "weave," was a free-flowing, crisscrossing offensive style that would permit his players to be creative. It was a loose system which allowed for a lot of improvisation, or "sophisticated pond hockey," as he would call it. It was an amalgam of the rough North American style with the wide open passing European game, and it required a lot of discipline.

"When we played, hockey was a north-and-south game," recalled Mike Eruzione, a winger from Boston University. "You stayed on your wing. Once you got over the red line, you'd dump it in the zone. Herb would say, 'You worked so hard to get the puck. Why would you just give it right back to them?' "

Brooks pushed the kids relentlessly. He watched their diet, had them do dry-land training to work on their footwork and flexibility, and drove them like they had never been driven before. He challenged them and pushed them beyond what they thought they were capable of. He was their motivator, their teacher, their psychologist and their father — all wrapped up into one. And, he was their worst nightmare, never cutting them any slack along the way.

In early September, the team began as challenging an exhibition schedule as had ever been organized for an American Olympic squad. Brooks figured the overseas tour would test them both mentally and physically right out of the gates. Beginning with an initial trip to Scandinavia, the team would go on to play a gruelling 61-game pre-Olympic schedule against some of the toughest foreign, collegiate and professional teams in the world.

The next step was to unify the boys and to start the long process of building team chemistry. Nobody was better at this than Brooks. He had a master plan and it all started and stopped with him. You see, many of the players came from rival schools and had played against each other in college. There was some genuine bad blood there, especially between the Boston kids and the Minnesota kids, who had squared off plenty of times over the past couple of years in the NCAA playoffs. Remember, in the late 1970s, the players didn't wear facemasks. So, if a player took a cheap shot or did something disrespectful, he usually had to drop the gloves to defend his actions. There had been some scraps over the years and those memories were still fresh.

At first there was some animosity about which players would be starting at what positions and how much playing time certain players were going to get. There was also a lot of animosity between the two factions with regards to how Brooks was going to treat the kids from Minnesota. After all, 16 of the 26 players hailed from the Land of 10,000 Lakes and the east coast kids just figured that Brooks would be a homer and give his kids all the top line positions.

But boy, oh boy, were they wrong. Brooks surely had a good chuckle over that thought. So, he put those ideas to rest pretty early on in the process by just treating everybody like crap, *especially* the Minnesota kids. There would be no favorites in this regime. If one screwed up, they all screwed up — and they were all going to skate like hell... without pucks, and for long periods of time. Brooks was going to be the alpha male in this pack, that was just understood.

Brooks wanted to make sure that there were absolutely no stars on his team. His strategy was to deflect all of their criticism and make himself the common enemy, thus uniting the players by default. Whereas the Minnesota kids were feuding with the east coast kids, now they would come together and make Brooks their common enemy. It was a radical concept, but it worked, because in no time all of the players truly detested him.

"There was a lot of ego and selfishness on the team," Brooks would later say. "So I became the lightning rod for their animosity. They forgot all about their differences with each other before long though and instead focused it on me."

Before long the squad was playing well, especially against the minor league teams from the Central Hockey League. Brooks had somehow been able to structure a deal with the professional minor league circuit to make it so their games actually counted in the standings. Because of that, they faced some really fierce competition. Remember, there weren't nearly as many NHL teams back then as there are now, so those CHL teams had some quality players who could've played in the NHL. And, they couldn't take the night off against the college kids either, which made for some epic battles between the two.

Facing competition like that night in and night out, the team got pretty good in a hurry. And, as long as the team was based in Minnesota, Brooks even scheduled exhibition games against the University of Minnesota, the NHL's Minnesota North Stars, and even the Warroad Lakers, a legendary men's senior team. The fans appreciated it and the players loved the diverse mix of talent and competition.

Throughout the course of it all, Brooks continued to hammer home his message of "team first." He would take players aside and remind them of his expectations that he had for them and then hold them accountable. He disciplined his players on a regular basis, seemingly never allowing them to ever get even a little bit overconfident. He was always reminding them that six of them were going to be cut in order to get the roster down to 20 players. He let that hang over them as a motivational tactic, and it worked big-time.

"I put them in deeper and deeper water all the time," Brooks would say. "To keep them in over their heads."

The team eventually went on a three week exhibition tour back across the pond, playing some of the top pro teams from Scandinavia and throughout Europe. During this time Brooks was still steering clear of getting close to any of his players. He didn't want to be their friend and he made that very clear. He wanted to be their coach. He knew that he had to cut several of these kids and didn't want it to become personal. His motivational tactics were pretty simple at this stage: "Skate like hell or you're off the team. No pro contract. No big money. No nothing..."

Being overseas and away from the States was good for the team's morale. Some of the regional cliques were broken down over there and the players began to bond. The experience for the players was summed up well in the book "One Goal," by John Powers and Arthur Kaminsky: "Europe would be an ideal place to start, to develop the camaraderie Brooks wanted to see. The food would be strange, the faces unfamiliar, the languages alien. Nobody would know a Gopher from a Badger in The Hague. They would merely be 26 kids in USA jerseys lugging their gear through a different hotel lobby every morning."

Brooks was determined to figure out why the Russians were the best conditioned athletes in the world. Knowing that he needed to take drastic measures in order to get his players to perform at that same level, he set out on a mission to better understand world class athletes and the conditioning regimens that they went through. He spoke to countless athletes and meticulously interviewed them, quizzing them about everything from pre-stretch warm-ups to nutritional supplements. He then consulted coaches of other international sports, such as soccer, track and swimming, and learned about aerobics, anaerobics, underloading, overloading, pulse rates, cardiovascular conditioning and flexibility exercises. He became consumed with it.

His ultimate goal was to teach his players the European game, supplementing the ingrained, physical North American style with a fluid passing and skating scheme. He knew that the players he had chosen, who were highly educated and open-minded individuals, would be up for trying anything and everything. From late night work-outs after practices,

71

to dry-land training in hotel parking lots, the players were pushed past the limits of normal humans. In Finland, he even had them working out in a soccer field, where they could visualize and work on their flexibility and finesse. Brooks' methods of motivation were radical and even revolutionary, but also very effective.

One of his former players and later a business partner, Paul Ostby, summed it up this way: "We have a tendency in our society as coaches and as people that when things are going well, we pat people on the back and say 'great job, way to go.' Then, conversely, when things are going poorly, we get real negative. Herbie was just the polar opposite of that. For him it was all about reverse psychology. So, when things were going well, that is when he put the heat on and asked for more — because that is when an athlete or a person is most receptive to that kind of psychology. Then, when things were going poorly, he would back off."

Brooks was able to get almost every one of his players to want to quit; to throw in the towel and raise the white flag. But then, somehow, at about the time that they had reached their breaking point, he would back off. And then he might even thrown in a compliment, just to completely throw them off guard. He knew which buttons to push on which players and when. It was amazing, considering he was constantly doing this with 26 different personalities. He knew which players he could yell and scream at and which ones he couldn't. He was an incredible judge of character and could read people very quickly.

A great example of this was captured by noted Sports Illustrated columnist E.M. Swift, who chronicled the team back in 1980: "The first time Brooks saw Silk skate at the Colorado Springs training camp, he took him aside and said, 'I don't know if you can't skate or if you won't skate, but I intend to find out,' wrote Swift. Silk had been an All-America at Boston University and had the reputation of playing his best in the biggest games. Brooks wanted him on the Olympic team, but he knew that Silk needed more speed. So he promised to ride him, to embarrass him, to rant and rave at him all season long. And even then, Brooks implied, he'd probably be too slow. For three months Brooks gave Silk not one single word of encouragement. 'Silk, you're too damn slow!' Then one day in practice the team was warming up, skating around the rink, when Silk heard, 'Keep at it, your skating's getting better.' He looked around and saw Brooks. 'He never even looked at me,' Silk said. 'He kind of whispered it on the way by. It made me feel so good I wanted to skate around and holler.' "

As the team progressed over the ensuing months, Brooks continued his philosophy of never really allowing his players to feel too good about themselves. One incident in particular that highlighted his temperament came in the Fall of 1979, when the team wound up tying a game against a professional club in Norway. The players were getting complacent and didn't seem to mind skating to a 4-4 stalemate against an inferior team. After the game was over and the teams had shaken hands, the players skated over to the exit to head down to the locker room.

That was when Brooks cut them off and told them to line up, they were going to skate some "Herbies." So, they skated, and skated, and then skated some more. In fact, he skated them so long that the arena manager finally shut off the lights on them and went home. Guys were puking and almost passing out. Even the team's general manager, Craig Patrick, thought that Brooks might kill somebody. That was when Herbie really started working them.

Bill Baker recalled it this way: "Herbie was really upset over how poorly we played," he said. "So, after we shook hands with the other team, Herbie says, 'stay on the ice gentlemen...' Well, he proceeds to start skating us right then and there. We are skating laps and sprints and he is just working us. I remember the east coast guys couldn't believe what was happening. They were absolutely dumfounded that their coach would actually make them skate after a game. Well, for the Minnesota guys, it was like no big deal. I mean, after all, this was Herbie, and we had seen this plenty of times before. I remember Buzzy Schneider, who had gotten kicked out of the game earlier, had been up in the stands but had to get redressed again and join us too. What was so funny was as we were skating around, the Norwegian fans stuck around because they thought we were putting on some sort of an American skating clinic. They were clapping up in the stands and that just made Herbie even madder by the minute. We all had to fight back the smiles over that one, but that was Herbie."

When it was all said and done, it had become a hallmark moment for the team. Sure, they were mad as hell at Herbie, but they had come together as a team. It was them vs. Herbie and they were determined to stick together and not be beaten. Brooks knew that he was going to have to be the enemy and that was all a part of his master plan. It was going to be lonely, but he knew in his heart that this was the

1980
UNITED STATES OLYMPIC HOCKEY TEAM
XIII WINTER OLYMPICS
GOLD MEDALIST

Front Row (L-R) Steve Janaszak, Bill Baker, Mark Johnson, Craig Patrick (Ass't Coach/Ass't GM), Mike Eruzione (Captain), Herb Brooks (Head Coach), Buzz Schneider, Jack O'Callahan, Jim Craig

Middle Row (L-R) Bob Suter, Rob McClanahan, Mark Wells, Bud Kessel (Equipment Manager), V. George Nagobads (Physician), Gary Smith (Trainer), Robert Fleming (Chairman), Ralph Jasinski (General Manager), Warren Strelow (Goalkeeping Coach), Bruce Horsch, Neal Broten, Mark Pavelich

Back Row (L-R) Phil Verchota, Steve Christoff, Les Auge, Dave Delich, Jack Hughes, Ken Morrow, Mike Ramsey, Dave Christian, Ralph Cox, Dave Silk, John Harrington, Eric Strobel only way he could break them down and then build them back up into Olympic champions.

"It was a lonely year for me," said Brooks to Sports Illustrated. "Very lonely. But it was by design. I never was close to my university players because they were so young. But this team had everything I wanted to be close to, everything I admired: the talent, the psychological makeup, the personality. But I had to stay away. If I couldn't know all, I didn't want to know one, because there wasn't going to be any favoritism."

As the Winter Games drew closer, Brooks was pleased with his team's progression. They had taken to his new system and were thriving in it. He would never tell them that, however, because then they would think he was satisfied — which he clearly wasn't. Then, to really shake things up in what some thought was a final act of motivational madness, Brooks did the unthinkable. With just a few games remaining in their exhibition schedule and the Opening Ceremonies just two weeks away, Brooks pulled his team captain, Mike Eruzione, aside and told him that he was going to cut him. He said he was a great captain and a good guy, but that it was a business decision. He didn't feel that he was playing up to his abilities and wanted to bring in a few new players to audition for his roster spot. Eruzione's jaw nearly hit the floor.

When the news finally spread throughout the rank and file that Brooks was serious about cutting the team captain, they all took notice

that none of their jobs were safe. By this point there were still 22 players on the roster and the team needed to get down to 20 in just a matter of days. Nobody was safe and Brooks would make them all sweat it out. True to his words, Brooks turned up the heat a little more and brought in two goal-scoring snipers from the University of Minnesota, Tim Harrer and Aaron Broten. The players were speechless.

They met up with the team, were given practice jerseys and told that they had as good a chance to make the squad as any man out there. It was particularly awkward for Neal Broten, a shoe-in to make the squad, to see his little brother show up amidst so much controversy. He tried to steer clear of all of it, but it was tough. Right away, all of the Minnesota vs. New England issues resurfaced and things got tense.

Finally, after a few days of practicing, all of the players rallied together and came to talk to their coach about what was going on. "This isn't fair," they said. "We've been through too much together and made too many sacrifices for you to bring in new players at this stage of the game, no way." Standing shoulder to shoulder, led by Eruzione and Jack O'Callahan, the players gave Brooks an ultimatum of their own. They said that unless he chose the final roster spots from the guys standing in the room right then and there, they were going to all quit. Brooks, seeing that they had unified and had become a family of sorts, backed off. They had passed his final test with flying colors.

With that, Brooks sent the two new players home and then proceeded to cut Harvard defenseman Jack Hughes, followed by New Hampshire forward Ralph Cox a short while later. They would be the final roster cuts. They were together at the time in an apartment back in the Twin Cities. Cutting Cox was tough for Brooks, who knew exactly how he felt at that moment. Brooks, of course, got the same call from his coach, Jack Riley, 20 years earlier, letting him know that he had been the last man cut from the 1960 U.S. Olympic team.

"He was such a gentleman that I cried on it," Brooks would later say. "I had a little flash-back of myself at the time. And you know what he told me? True story. He said, 'That's all right, coach, I understand. You guys are going to win the gold medal.' Ralph Cox said that. And when we won it, that's who I thought of, Ralph Cox."

Meanwhile, Eruzione, the emotional team leader, dug deep after his little wake up call and promptly went out and tallied five goals in the team's last three exhibition games. After 57 games and buckets of blood, sweat and tears, he finished strong and made a statement. He was a survivor. Brooks knew that he had gotten the message loud and clear. Mission accomplished.

"I will never forget when he called me into his office and just flat out said he was going to cut me," said Eruzione. "Actually, he said he would say that I hurt my back or something so I could still travel with the team as an assistant coach and come to Lake Placid. He was always playing with your mind a little bit, and I wasn't sure what he was up to at that moment. He was trying to see how close the team was and it might have been the last hurdle that he placed in front of me. I mean the guys were pissed off that he would consider cutting one of us and bring in new players from the outside. We rallied together though and that united us. His thought was to get everybody against him so that we would all be on the same page. He was just a very demanding coach and could be difficult to play for, but you couldn't argue with the results. He was like your dad. I mean sometimes you loved your dad and sometimes you hated him because he made you do things you didn't want to do. That was Herb."

There was still one lesson in humility that the coach had up his sleeve and that was going to be revealed in the team's final exhibition game at the famed Madison Square Garden in New York City. Just four days prior to the lighting of the caldron of the XIIIth Winter Olympic Games, Brooks had scheduled one last tune-up for his boys. Only this one wasn't a cream-puff opponent from Liechtenstein, it was arguably the best hockey team the world had ever seen, the Soviet Union. The Soviets had dominated Olympic hockey for the past 20 years and were simply unstoppable. In fact, they had won four straight gold medals and had not lost a single Olympic contest since 1968. They had even recently pummeled the National Hockey League All-Star team by the lopsided score of 6-0. Even the top NHL players were shocked at just how good the Russians actually were.

Before the game started, while the players were skating warm-up laps, the Americans looked completely in awe.

"When they came out on the ice, our players were applauding," remembered Brooks, "that's when I knew we were in trouble."

The Soviets' reputation as hardened, stoic soldiers created an aura of invincibility around them. In the end, the Russians took it easy on the young Americans, beating them just 10-3. It was the perfect slap

ON THE OLYMPICS...

"The Olympic Games are about one man or one woman; about dreamers; about the pursuit of perfection. Dan Jansen, a former gold medal Olympic speed skater, said 'I don't try to beat anybody, I just try to beat myself.'

"The Olympics have goals: to promote the physical and moral qualities of the athletes; to promote peace; and to spread goodwill. With those things a certain brotherhood and international understanding exists. That cooperation develops in an environment that preserves the dignity and values of sports.

"The interlocking rings, the qualities that they stand for, represent the most prestigious sporting organization in the world. There are no losers, only winners, because everybody represents excellence. The Olympic Games have taught me that obstacles exist to be overcome, to believe in a better tomorrow, and to make sacrifices for the unknown."
— *Herb Brooks*

76

in the face Brooks wanted for his kids though. He didn't want them to be too cocky heading into the Games, and, more importantly, he didn't want the Soviets to think twice about being able to beat a bunch of college kids. Brooks knew that the Soviets would overlook his team. He knew that they were complacent and that they were ripe to be beaten. Herb knew it deep in his gut. Now all he had to do was somehow convince his players of it.

"BROOKSISMS"

Original sayings, as told by Herb Brooks... and retold by 1980 Olympians John Harrington, Dave Silk and Mike Eruzione:

"You're playing worse every day, and right now you're playing like it is next week..."

"Gentlemen, you don't have enough talent to win on talent alone..."

"You look like you have a five pound fart on your head..."

"Hey Ref, you should take a two week vacation and then retire..."

"I am going to be your coach but I am not going to be your friend..."

"It's confusion by design, but there's a method to our madness..."

"Gentlemen, let's not be a whore out there..."

"If you make a mistake out there, make it by co-mission instead of by o-mission..."

"We're going to climb into their jockstraps out there..."

"In front of the net, it's bloody nose alley..."

"Boys, I'm asking you to go to the well again..."

"There's a fine line between guts and brains..."

"Throw the puck back and weave, but don't just weave for the sake of weaving..."

"Let's be idealistic, but let's be practical..."

"Let's cut their throats gentlemen..."

"You can't be common, the common man goes nowhere; you have to be uncommon..."

"If you want to bring a hard hat and lunch pail to work, that is fine with me..."

"You see the tiger, you walk up to him, spit in his eye, and then shoot em'..."

"Play well here, and it's money in your back pocket..."

CH. 8) EVERY NOW AND THEN, IT'S OK TO TAKE A LEAP OF FAITH; THAT'S WHEN MIRACLES CAN HAPPEN

With his team unified and ready to make the trip to Lake Placid, Brooks knew that he had trained and prepared his players to the best of his abilities. Now he would need to convince them that despite their young age and lack of experience, that they were capable of winning the gold medal. He knew that the Soviets were ripe for defeat and that his boys were ready to take that leap of faith to a place they had never been before. He would need to push them harder than they had ever been pushed before though, because it was there, and only there, where they would ultimately achieve what had previously been considered impossible.

With an impressive 42-16-3 exhibition record, the team then headed to Lake Placid, where they would embark on their epic journey towards Olympic gold. Most figured that bronze was a long shot and that silver was improbable. Gold, however, gold was an impossibility. That belonged to the Russians. Herbie had other ideas though and was about to make history. Though seeded seventh in the 12-nation pool, the Americans felt that they had something to prove.

Finally, after all the pomp and circumstance surrounding the Opening Ceremonies, Team USA took on Sweden in the opening game. The Americans were visibly tentative and nervous, and came out flat to start the game. By the end of the period the Swedes had out-shot them, 16-7, and led 1-0. Brooks had come too far to let his boys falter in their opening game and decided to take immediate action. So, in the dressing room following the first period, he went on a tirade. It was all premeditated though, of course. He slammed open the door and quickly noticed Robbie McClanahan with his skates off and an ice pack on his thigh. He was suffering from severe cramping and had been told by one of the trainers that he was done for the evening. Brooks went berserk.

Perhaps famed Sports Illustrated writer E.M. Swift summed up the chaotic scene best in his Dec. 29, 1980, article which chronicled the event: *"A reminder of what we can be."*

"You gutless son of a bitch! Nobody's going belly-up now!", Brooks screamed. "Instead of coming in and yelling at us as a team, he picked on Robbie," recalled Mark Johnson. "It was the craziest locker room I've ever been in. He's swearing. Everyone else is swearing. Robbie's swearing and crying. Then Robbie follows him out into the hall and is screaming at him. 'I'll show you!' And in a minute here's the door flying open again and Herbie's coming back yelling, 'It's about time you grew up, you baby...' "

"At that point Johnson yelled at Eruzione to get Brooks out of there. Can you beat that? The star player was yelling at the captain to get the coach out of the locker room. Finally, Jack O'Callahan, a defenseman who wasn't dressed for the game because of an injury, grabbed Brooks from behind; Brooks and McClanahan were jawbone to jawbone and O'Callahan was afraid they'd start swinging. Mean-while, the rest of the team was sitting there thinking, 'We're one period into the Olympics, down one lousy goal, and the couch loses his marbles.' "

Apparently, that was just the wake-up call Brooks' boys would need though. McClanahan, now mad as hell, got redressed and went back onto the ice for the second period. There, the Americans out-shot the Swedes and tied the game at one apiece. McClanahan, meanwhile, couldn't even sit down between shifts because his leg was in too much pain to even bend it. So he stood the entire period, rooting his teammates on from his post — which, not coincidentally, was about as far away from Herbie as possible.

The Americans fell behind just minutes into the third period, but then rallied back late in the third after Brooks pulled goalie Jim Craig from the net in order to add an additional attacker. Then, with just 27 seconds remaining in the game, Bill Baker took a Mark Pavelich centering pass and found the back of the net to give the U.S. an emotional, yet critical, 2-2 tie.

Team trainer Gary Smith remembered the infamous incident

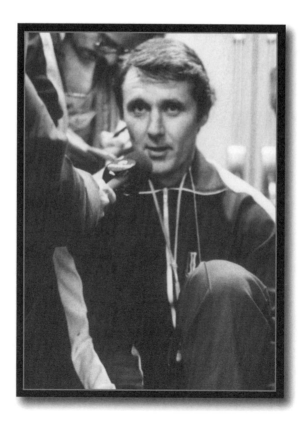

this way: "You know, there was always somebody to kind of calm things down after Herbie ripped em' a new one, and one of those guys was Robbie McClanahan," he said. "Herbie picked him for that role because he knew that he could handle it. I remember playing against Sweden, it was the first period and Robbie bruised his thigh pretty badly. So I took him back to ice it in the locker room. Herbie then came in after the period and went after him like there was no tomorrow. He called him the biggest pussy that ever walked the earth and that he wasn't tough enough to play in the National Hockey League."

"Robbie, meanwhile, has a huge wrap around his leg, and he jumps up and goes after Herbie. The ice bag flies off and the two of them are screaming at each other out in the hall. The Swedes are right next door in the next locker room and are wondering what the hell is going on. So, Herbie brings him back into our locker room and is reading him the riot act. I am standing there thinking 'Oh my God, we are at the Olympics and Herb has lost it!'. And as I thought that, I looked around the room. I could see that every one of Robbie's teammates getting more and more pissed off at Herbie over the way he was treating him. So, they rallied together and went out and beat the Swedes, just to spite him. Herbie, however, was a psychology major, and knew that all along. He sold his theory to his players and they bought it. He just knew how to deal with people in his own way, and that was the secret to his success."

Baker's goal, meanwhile, acted as a catalyst for the young Americans, who then upset Czechoslovakia, and the amazing Stastny brothers, 7-3, thanks to goals from Mark Pavelich, Buzz Schneider, Phil Verchota and, yes, Rob McClanahan — bum leg and all. Brooks became a household name shortly after that too when, during that game, he threatened to shove a stick down a Czech player's throat after he cheapshotted an American player at the buzzer. The whole incident was caught on TV and the American fans loved it. It showed that we weren't going to take any crap and that we were tough. The country was now taking notice and starting to root for these guys.

After beating both Norway and Romania, now only West Germany stood in the way of Team USA getting into the medal round. In that game the Americans found themselves down 2-0 in the first, only to see McClanahan and Broten each tally to tie it up. McClanahan then scored again on another breakaway in the third, and Phil Verchota tallied late to give the U.S. a 4-2 win.

There was now a buzz about these nameless, faceless hockey players, but nobody knew who they were. And that too was by design. You see, Brooks had forbidden them to participate in the post-game press conferences. He didn't care who he offended, he wasn't about to put individuals ahead of the team. That had been his philosophy from Day One and that wasn't about to change. The media room could only accommodate three players at time and Brooks figured that the press would only want to talk to the team's three best players. He saw that as a potentially divisive situation, so he decided to deny all press requests for his players.

"I did not want a 'I,' 'Me,' 'Myself' organization, instead I wanted it to be all about 'We, "Us' and 'Ourselves,' " said Brooks. "If we started taking people out of the locker room and taking them down to press conferences, then we would start breaking down that togetherness we had worked so hard to achieve. The press was mad as hell, especially the American press. The European press, they understood a little bit more. But anyway I was in trouble. They referred to me as 'Ayatollah Brooks' and that I was holding the players as hostages. That was something else, let me tell you."

Ultimately, to make the Olympic committee officials happy, Brooks attended the press conferences by himself. Then, when the reporters got upset and accused him of trying to steal the limelight from his players, he stopped showing up altogether and sent his general manager, Craig Patrick, in his place. This, of course, really pissed them off, which, in turn, made Herbie chuckle even more. He didn't need his kids worrying about the added pressures of what to say to the press, he needed them worrying about their next game. And that next game was a big one. The Russians were now all that stood between the Americans and a medal. It was going to be the biggest game of their lives.

The Americans, with a very respectable record of 4-0-1, now had the formidable task of trying to dethrone the mighty Soviets. Led by Vladislav Tretiak, the world's premier goaltender, they had already outscored their opponents in the tournament by the ridiculous margin of 51-11 through their first five games. Yes, this squad was just another of a long line of dynasty teams which had won the last four Olympic golds, and five of the last six. In fact, the only team to beat them since 1956 was the United States, back in 1960.

The day before the big game, Brooks came in to talk to his boys

after practice. He told them that the "Russians were ripe to be beat; that they were lethargic changing their lines; and that their passes had lost their crispness." All season long it had been a running joke between Brooks and his players that the star of the team, Boris Mikhailov, a 13-year tenured captain, looked like Stan Laurel. Little by little he had been trying to break down the Soviet mystique in terms that the kids could relate to. Everybody knew that Laurel and Hardy were a couple of buffoons, and that was exactly how he wanted his players to feel about their opponents that next night. Sure, the Soviets were technically superior to any team in the world. They were faster, stronger and better in nearly every way. Every way but one, they lacked heart, and that was something Brooks was hoping to capitalize on.

The game had so many political and social implications surrounding it too. There was the Iranian hostage crisis; the recent Soviet invasion of Afghanistan; the fact that the U.S. economy was in disarray with interest rates and inflation soaring; there were long gas lines from coast to coast; and there was the realization that President Carter had already announced an American boycott of the upcoming Summer Olympics in Moscow. The stakes were enormous and our nation's pride was at stake. It was us vs. them, the "red menace," on an international stage. Talk about pressure.

The Soviets and their imposing red sweaters with CCCP emblazoned on their chests, hit the ice looking like stoic, expressionless robots. They were Red Army soldiers and did what they were told. It was their job to win gold medals and they were simply going to work. They had played together for years, some as many as 15 together, and were not about to be frazzled by a bunch of college kids. The Soviets had hockey down to a science. Their approach to the game was fundamentally different than ours. To build cohesiveness, their coaching staff would always take an entire forward line from one of their club teams, such as the Red Army or Dynamo Moscow, and elevate it as a whole to the Soviet National team for International competition. That was why the Petrov, Kharlamov and Mikhailov line was so incredibly good. They had been playing side by side for more than a decade together. Talk about chemistry. The Americans, meanwhile, had always just slapped together all-star lines, thinking that they could build continuity overnight. Fundamentally, the two programs were polar opposites, but Brooks had been trying to change all of that over the past six months.

In the locker room just before the game that Friday, Brooks reminded his players that the Soviets were already looking past them and on to the gold medal game. He told them that the Soviets didn't respect the American players or the American way of life. He reminded them that their 10-3 Madison Square Garden defeat was a lifetime ago. He told them that the American people were behind them and that they were about to make history. He told them that he believed in them and that he was proud of how far they had come.

Then, just as he was about to leave, he reached into his pocket and pulled out a little scrap of yellow paper. He opened it up and looked into the eyes of all of his players sitting before him. The room was quiet with nervous anticipation. He then read it aloud: "You were born to be a player. You were meant to be here. This moment is yours." And then he simply walked out of the room. It was go time.

"It's David against Goliath, and I hope we remember to bring our slingshots," Brooks would say.

With that, the puck was dropped and the game roared back and forth with lightening speed. The "Iron Range Line" of Mark Pavelich, John Harrington and Buzz Schneider got the Americans on the board first, when, down 1-0, Pavelich fed Schneider for a nice slap shot which found the top corner. The Russians answered back three minutes later, only to see Mark Johnson tie it up with just seconds to go in the period on a nice open ice steal and break-away. When they returned to the ice following the intermission, the U.S. team was shocked to see that Soviet coach Victor Tikhanov had replaced Tretiak in goal with backup goal-tender Vladimir Myshkin. He was upset about him letting in the soft goal at the buzzer and wanted to punish him for it. While it would appear that the great bear was wounded, the Soviets came back to take the lead, having now out-shot the Americans, 30-10, through two periods. Goalie Jim Craig was playing huge though and his teammates were feeding off of that emotion. Johnson then got his second tally of the game at 8:39 of the third period to tie it at 3-3.

Then, midway through the third period, Schneider dumped the

puck into the Russian zone and Harrington dug it out to his old UM-Duluth wingmate, Mark Pavelich. Pavelich then floated a perfect pass to the top of the circle where Mike Eruzione fired home "the shot heard 'round the world." Eruzione leaped into the air with excitement and literally ran across the ice to celebrate with his linemates. It was utter pandemonium at the arena as the crowd went crazy. They had somehow taken the lead, but could they hold it?

The final 10 minutes of the game were arguably the longest in U.S. hockey history, but the Americans somehow held on behind Jim Craig's brilliant netminding down the stretch. The players took extremely short shifts but remained calm and didn't panic. Herbie's tough training regimen had finally paid off when it truly mattered the most. All of those "Herbies" suddenly made sense now.

Ironically, in the end it was the Soviet players, not the Americans, who reverted back to the old North American dump-and-chase style of undisciplined hockey that Brooks always wanted to stay away from. They didn't even pull their goalie in the final minutes, probably because they didn't know how. They had never lost before! The final moments were breath taking.

Then, as the crowd counted down the final seconds, famed television announcer Al Michaels shouted *"Do you believe in miracles...Yes!"* The horn sounded and the crowd erupted. It was a venerable sea of American flags. Our boys had done it. The players rejoiced at center ice in a heap of red, white and blue insanity. Players were crying and the fans were crying right along with them. Brooks' boys had somehow done the impossible. And with that, the Americans had made it into the gold medal game.

After the players were through celebrating on the ice, they shook hands with the Russian players. The Americans then retreated back to

their locker room. There, it was eerily silent. The gravity of just what they had accomplished hadn't sunk in yet. A few guys cried but most of the others sat quietly, almost shell shocked. The moment was surreal. Then, out of the blue, somebody started singing *"God Bless America."* Before long, all 20 players were humming along. It turns out the reason they were humming, however, was because nobody knew the words. Nobody cared, they were on top of the world.

"I get asked a lot if I had thought of that line ahead of time, and the answer is no," recalled Al Michaels. "It just came to me at that very moment. My first concern at the time, to tell you the truth, was to just call the game correctly and make sure that the play-by-play was precise and mechanically right on. I will never forget those final moments as the clock wound down though, it was almost surreal. The puck came out to

THE 1980 U.S. OLYMPIC TEAM ROSTER

NAME	HOMETOWN	COLLEGE
Bill Baker (D)	Grand Rapids, Minn.	University of Minnesota
Neal Broten (F)	Roseau, Minn.	University of Minnesota
Dave Christian (D)	Warroad, Minn.	University of North Dakota
Steve Christoff (F)	Richfield, Minn.	University of Minnesota
Jim Craig (G)	North Easton, Mass.	Boston University
Mike Eruzione (F)	Winthrop, Mass.	Boston University
John Harrington (F)	Virginia, Minn.	University of Minn.-Duluth
Steve Janaszak (G)	White Bear Lake, Minn.	University of Minnesota
Mark Johnson (F)	Madison, Wis.	University of Wisconsin
Rob McClanahan (F)	St. Paul, Minn.	University of Minnesota
Ken Morrow (D)	Flint, Mich.	Bowling Green University
Jack O'Callahan (D)	Charlestown, Mass.	Boston University
Mark Pavelich (F)	Eveleth, Minn.	University of Minn.-Duluth
Mike Ramsey (D)	Minneapolis, Minn.	University of Minnesota
Buzz Schneider (F)	Babbitt, Minn.	University of Minnesota
Dave Silk (F)	Scituate, Mass.	Boston University
Eric Strobel (F)	Rochester, Minn.	University of Minnesota
Bob Suter (D)	Madison, Wis.	University of Wisconsin
Phil Verchota (F)	Duluth, Minn.	University of Minnesota
Mark Wells (F)	St. Claire Shores, Mich.	Bowling Green University

MANAGEMENT	HOMETOWN	TITLE
Herb Brooks	St. Paul, Minn.	Head Coach
Craig Patrick	Wellesley, Mass.	Assistant Coach
Ralph Jasinski	Mounds View, Minn.	Manager
Warren Strelow	Mahtomedi, Minn.	Goalie Coach
Dr. V.G. Nagobads	Edina, Minn.	Physician
Gary Smith	Minneapolis, Minn.	Trainer
Bud Kessel	St. Paul, Minn.	Equipment Manager

center ice with about six seconds to go and all of a sudden there was that moment where you realized that it was over. So, at that moment the first thing that popped into my mind was the word miraculous. From there, miraculous just came out in the form of a question. So, I answered it. *'Do you believe in Miracles?... YES!'*. Then I just shut up and soaked it all in for a few minutes. Anything I would have said after that would have been superfluous. I mean there was nothing left to say and I wanted the pictures to tell the story at that point. To be honest, I didn't even remember saying it at the time. When I saw the replay and saw how it just fit the moment perfectly, then I knew that it was going to be pretty special."

Meanwhile, where was Herbie while all of this was going on? Would you believe in the bathroom? That's right. He wanted the boys to enjoy their moment and to stay out of the way for a little while, to let them think about what they had done and to reflect on what it had taken them all to get to that point. He eventually came back into the locker room though and put things into perspective in a hurry.

Herbie, ever the psychologist, quickly put the players back in their place. He screamed at them not to get too cocky, and that they hadn't won anything yet. The next day at practice, Brooks put the team through a grueling workout, constantly reinforcing to his men that they had proven nothing up to that point. He challenged them and asked them if they would be satisfied with silver. This, of course, was all part of his master plan, to get the players to further despise him, and force them to rally amongst themselves and become even stronger for their final game together.

In the gold medal game that Sunday morning, the U.S. would face Finland, a team which had beaten the Czechs in the other semifinal. Sure, they weren't as good as the Russians, but they were an outstanding team nonetheless and were not to be taken lightly. The players were loose during the pre-game in the locker room. In fact, they were probably a little too loose. When Brooks walked in and saw guys autographing sticks, he went off. He started to throw things and he started in with the personal attacks.

"I knew this was all to good to be true," he screamed. "I knew you guys would get too cocky and blow it! They said you were too young and I guess they were right! You clearly don't have enough talent to beat the Finns!" The players had heard it all before, but this time they knew it was going to be the last time. So, they got real serious about what they needed to accomplish.

With that, they hit the ice knowing it would be their last time together. They had come a long way and did not want to settle for silver. Despite being down early in the second period, Steve Christoff got the Americans on the board at the 4:39 mark with a nice wrister down low. The Finns hung tough, however, and went into the third period up 2-1. Brooks then gave an emotional speech just before they took the ice for the third and final period, saying "that if they lost this game that they would take it to their f---ing graves!" He walked away and then came back where he repeated it again, "Your f---ing graves!" The players got it.

They had come this far and would regret it for the rest of their collective lives if they somehow let it slip away. So, they came out possessed. The constant reminder of Herbie saying "Play your game... Play your game," was comforting to the players, who knew that they were on the verge of making history.

Starting the rally back was Phil Verchota, who took a Dave Christian pass in the left circle and found the back of the net at 2:25. With that, the Americans started to smell blood and immediately went for the jugular. Just three minutes later, Robbie McClanahan scored off a Mark Johnson pass to give the U.S. a 3-2 lead. Johnson then saved the day by adding a short-handed backhander of his own just minutes later to give the U.S. a two-goal cushion. From there, Jim Craig just hung on for the final few minutes of the game. The players on the bench banged their sticks on the boards as they counted down the last 10 seconds. Al Michaels this time screamed: *"This impossible dream, comes true!"*

They believed in themselves and they did it. They had overcome the impossible and earned the right to be called the best in the world. And, like nearly every other game during the tournament, the team rallied from behind to win. They showed great character and great discipline, both hallmarks of Herb Brooks' coaching philosophy. In fact, in the seven games the team played, they were out-scored 9 goals to 6 in the first period, but then came back to outscore their opponents 16-3 in the third period. That was a true testament to Herbie's conditioning program, which emphasized having more stamina and energy than their opponents at the end of their games.

From there it was utter pandemonium and chaos as the players threw their sticks into the crowd and piled onto one another to the chants of "U-S-A! U-S-A!" Herbie, meanwhile, thrust his arm into the air in a brief moment of uncharacteristic jubilation and satisfaction, only to then sneak out the back door, leaving the players to celebrate their achievement amongst themselves. This was their time and he wanted them to enjoy it. The sight of Jim Craig searching for his father after the game with an American flag draped over his shoulder was priceless. His mother had recently passed away and it had been her dying wish to watch her son play in the Olympics.

Afterward, many of the players were visibly moved by what they had done, as evidenced during the singing of the National Anthem, when the entire team gathered on the top platform to sing the Star-Spangled Banner. Typically, just the team captain stands up there, but Eruzione waved all of his teammates over to join him for the uplifting celebration. They then marched around the rink in their matching blue sweat suits, singing, laughing and waving to the crowd. Yes, this was their time. And, more importantly, it was America's time.

The Soviets, however, were in a state of shock. They would wind up claiming the silver medal in the round robin tournament, but to them that was like coming in last place. Many just stood and watched the young American kids, singing, dancing and enjoying the moment. Deep down they were jealous as hell. Hockey wasn't like that for them It wasn't a game. For them hockey was a job. The Russians knew that back home waiting for them were their Communist government bosses, who were not going to be pleased. There were ramifications for losing and they knew it. Maybe that explains why when the team cleared out of their rooms at the Olympic Village, clean-up workers found more than 100 empty vodka bottles hidden above the ceiling panels.

The "Miracle on Ice," as it quickly became known as, will forever remain etched in our memories as one of the greatest sporting events of all-time. Looking back, it was achieved by enormous ambition, coupled with great passing, checking, speed, and sound puck control. Shrewdly, Brooks refused to play the typical dump-and-chase style of hockey that had been so prevalent in North American hockey. He was prepared and stuck to his game plan. He knew that when the opportunity presented itself, his team had to be ready to take advantage of it.

"They were really mentally tough and goal-oriented," said Brooks of the team. "They came from all different walks of life, many having competed against one another, but they came together and grew to be a real close team. I pushed this team really hard, I mean I really pushed them. But they had the ability to answer the bell. Our style of play was probably different than anything in North America. We adopted more of a hybrid style of play — a bit of the Canadian school and a little bit of the European school. The players took to it like ducks to water, and they really had a lot of fun playing it. We were a fast, creative team that played extremely disciplined without the puck. Throughout the Olympics, they had a great resiliency about them. I mean they came from behind six or seven times to win. They just kept on moving and working and digging. I think we were as good a conditioned team as there was in the world, outside maybe the Soviet Union. We got hot and lucky at the right times, and it was just an incredible experience for all of us."

As for the aftermath, it left a truly lasting legacy. A grateful nation, saddened by what was happening in the world, hailed the team as heroes. A visit to the White House followed, as well as appearances in cities across the land. Covers of Wheaties cereal boxes, magazines, awards, honors, speaking engagements and a whole lot of hoopla would follow for all the players. In the heart of the Cold War, beating the mighty Soviets was something bigger than they could've ever imagined. The country went crazy with a newly found sense of national pride, all thanks to the team's incredible achievement. Sports Illustrated went on to name the team, collectively, as "Sportsmen of the Year" and Life Magazine declared it as the "Sports Achievement of the Decade." It would later be named as the "Sports Achievement of the Century" by several major sources as well.

Sports Illustrated summed up the entire experience like this: "At a time when international tensions and domestic frustrations had damp-ened traditional American optimism, the underdog U.S. Olympic hock-ey team gave the entire nation a lift by defeating the world's top team, the Soviets, and ultimately winning the gold medal. Those youngsters did so by means of the old-fashioned American work ethic, which some people feared was disappearing from the land."

Looking back, the event was extremely significant for the growth of American hockey. The historic win brought hockey to the front-pages of newspapers everywhere, and forever opened the door to the NHL for American-born players from below the 49th parallel. The impact of the event was far reaching, and is still being felt today. Since that milestone game back in 1980, hockey in the United States has grown significantly at not only the professional and amateur levels, but also at the youth lev-els with both boys and girls. And, the fact that we now have NHL fran-chises in Arizona, North Carolina, Florida, California and Texas can all

be traced back, in part, to the legacy of Herb Brooks and the "Miracle on Ice."

That win over the Soviets in the semifinals, followed by the gold medal win over Finland were simply unforgettable. Even today, most Americans who were around back in 1980 can probably tell you precisely where they were and what they were doing at that exact moment in time. Like the lunar landing or even the assassination of JFK, it too will always have a meaningful place in our hearts and in our minds.

Fittingly, the team got to fly back to Minnesota on Air Force One. On the plane, Herbie and his family relaxed by going through bags and bags of telegrams, which had been plastered on the walls outside of the team locker room. Somebody had taken them all down and put them in grocery bags for everyone to sift through. Then, when they landed in Minneapolis, despite the fact that it was –30 below zero outside, the team was met by droves of adoring fans who had braved the elements to welcome them home as heroes. It was a fitting ending to a spectacular achievement.

Shortly thereafter, Brooks spoke candidly about the entire experience during a key-note speech to a group of business executives:

"To be honest with you, I feel our win was highly magnified because basically it occurred during a time when our country was searching for a source of national pride," he said. "The hostages in Iran, the Russian invasion of Afghanistan, spiraling inflation and climbing interest rates — all of those things combined to provide a climate that was made to order for our hockey team. All of a sudden, millions of Americans could sit in front of their TV sets and forget for a few moments about foreign affairs and the economy. Our hockey team had become a catalyst toward national pride."

"I think we all know it was only a hockey game. But if that's what it takes to get young people in this country to wave the flag and sing the National Anthem, instead of burning the flag and ridiculing this nation, then I'm awfully proud to have been a part of it. But in a very real sense, it wasn't my team, or the athletes' team. It belonged to this nation, it was 'America's Team,' with all due respect to the Dallas Cowboys, of course. Hey, the U.S. Olympic hockey team got eight write-in votes during the New Hampshire Primary. And if we'd had the Cowboy cheerleaders, we'd have probably gotten eight more!

"It's easy for me to joke about the team now, but about a year ago when we started putting the team together on paper, no one was laughing. As a matter of fact, hockey people were telling me all I had was a bunch of pretty figure skaters. You talk about pressure, how many of you would like to put your entire future in the hands of 18 and 20-year-old kids? Actually, after I was selected to coach the team, my first move was to form an advisory staff of good hockey people throughout the United States. We weighed the input and drew a composite list of our top candidates. Then came the really tough stuff.

"During April, May and June of last year we were able to get what we felt were the best 68 amateur players in the country to our training camp in Colorado Springs. That may sound easy, but remember, most of those young men have professional hockey in their futures. So we had to deal with professional agents and National Hockey League general managers to get those players into camp. After dealing with the players' agents, the NHL managers and the athletes themselves, I felt that I could have negotiated just about anything at that point.

"From those 68 players, we chose a squad of 26 and left for a 10-game swing of Finland and Norway. We won seven, lost two, tied one and returned home for what I feel was one of the most crucial tests for the team. Remember, we had 26 young men, which we would trim to 20 for the Olympics, and all were from different backgrounds, different environments and different personalities. We were a team of individuals. But, we knew that for us to be successful we would have to understand that each individual was different, yet he had to fit into our team style of play. Not only were these guys individuals in their own right, but most of them had been bitter rivals in the past. It was like trying to put Muhammad Ali and Howard Cosell in front of a TV camera and telling them to use just one microphone.

"The Central Hockey League though, provided us with the crucible of competition that allowed the individuals to come together as a team. We took that group of young men and played 60 games, 48 of which were on the road, with no mothers and fathers or girlfriends in the stands. The team played before indifferent, if not hostile, crowds. The Central Hockey League allowed us to play a 19-game schedule against their professionals, and to be sure that the teams didn't take the night off against us, the games all counted in the CHL standings. We won 14 of those 19 games and people quickly began to refer to us as a hockey team and not a bunch of figure skaters.

"By the time of the pre-Olympic tournament in December, we had managed to gel as a team. Not only had we converted young individuals into young team players, but we had given them a new style of play. Our approach to the game, our tactics, were entirely different. Our tactics were a combination of the best of the European system of finesse, and the North American system of knock-em-rock-em-hockey. We were intent on playing what I considered a positive way. Our objective was to break down the stereotypes. I wanted the players to have freedom to interchange positions, to be creative, yet to blend together as a team. Patience and timing were the two key ingredients.

"We had, I believe, the toughest pre-Olympic schedule of any U.S. hockey team ever, and we would be by far the youngest team when we entered the Olympic tournament. The month of January nearly killed us. We played 13 games in 26 days and finished the month a very tired and beat up hockey team. And as a fitting ending to that dismal month, we played the Russians in Madison Square Garden as a final tune-up. We went into that game a fatigued hockey team. We hadn't been playing well and there we were in Madison Square Garden, what a place. You have to take an elevator to the third floor to get on the ice. And I knew we were in trouble when the Russian players were introduced and I looked around and saw that our players were applauding. The game was supposed to start at two o'clock, but we didn't start playing until 3:30, an hour and a half later. We got our asses kicked. The Russians rolled over us, 10-3.

"Now we had a group of very disappointed young men heading towards Lake Placid, but we made that defeat work in our favor. A good team, a good athlete, or a good organization is never hurt by a good ass kicking. A good licking never hurts a quality team. So we went to Lake Placid, a controlled environment in the Olympic village, and our players were in awe. We told them 'Don't look at yourselves as the youngest team in the Olympic games; don't look at yourselves as the youngest team in American history; don't use your youthfulness as a liability — use it as an asset.' Youthfulness is desire, it's hungriness.

"We knew we had to turn our youth into a positive factor. We were picked seventh, and as all of you know, seventh place just isn't going to get you any kind of medal. Our goal was to get in the final four and we knew we had to skate well in our first two games against the Swedes and Czechs in order to have a chance. Well, we tied Sweden on a shot in the final 20 seconds and that started the ball rolling. We upset a good Czech team shortly thereafter, 7-3, and the momentum was firmly established. Our players were believing in themselves and believing in our system of play. They were euphoric over the tie and win in the first two games.

"I was getting scared. We still had some tough teams left. The Norwegians, Rumanians and West Germans weren't pushovers, but our players responded. They came from behind to beat Norway, skated past Romania, and scored another come-from-behind victory over West Germany. We had reached the final four. Our next game was with the Russians, who had just clobbered us in Madison Square Garden.

"I don't know if many of you realize it, but ABC tried to get the Olympic committee to move the game from 5:00 pm to 8:30 pm that night. You know, television can move a championship boxing match; it can put baseball players in thermal underwear for the World Series; and keep the Super Bowl in warm-weather cities. But the International Ice Hockey Federation told ABC that the show must go on, and it must go on at five o'clock.

"I don't think our team would have cared if we had played the game at midnight though. We had put all the pieces together and we were ready. Before the game I simply told the team: 'You were born to be a player. You were meant to be here. This moment is yours.' I told them that they were not going to be denied. I've got to be honest with you though, in the back of my mind I was saying 'Good Lord, this is a bunch of kids going out to play the world's greatest hockey team.' This is the same Russian team that had just beaten the National Hockey League All-Stars, and beaten them badly. This is a team of sports professionals. Russian teams have won five Olympic gold medals, 16 World Championships and 19 European Championships — and during those tournaments they had outscored their opposition 1,492 to 394. Eight of the players on this Russian team helped beat a group of National Hockey Leaguers in the legendary 1972 Summit Series. At that time, about 12 of our players were playing peewee hockey.

"As you know, we came from behind and beat them, 4-3. And, as they say, the rest is history. There was one particular moment after the victory that I would like to share with you though. While it was one of the greatest moments in my life, I was emotionally drained after the game. A few minutes after it was over I was led to a room filled with International Olympic Committee officials and ABC TV officials. They were all staring at a telephone. They said the President would be calling on that phone. Hell, by the way they were acting, you would have thought the President was in the room. They told me to pick up the phone when the little white light came on, and I did, but I heard a click on the line. The phone was dead.

"We had a bad connection, but the IOC and ABC officials didn't know that. So I leaned back in the chair and said: *'Jimmy... Jimmy, is that you? Yes. Thank you. Yes. We'll be at the White House, but we still have another game to play first. Jimmy, what kind of beer will you be serving? Billy Beer? That's fine Jimmy, just fine. And yes sir, I'll have my players go down first thing Monday morning and sign up for the draft.'* Well the Olympic and ABC officials were going crazy. They couldn't believe it. Finally, Al Michaels, the ABC Sportscaster, figured out what I had done and let them in on my little prank. He then proceeded to tell me a few things that you'll never hear on the air. It was a fun moment. Then, when I did speak to the President, that was a great moment too, for all of us.

"I then told our players before the Finland game for the gold medal two nights later that it would be our last event together. This would be our best; our last would be the best. They proved me right. I think U.S. Senator David Durenberger, from the state of Minnesota, put our accomplishment in excellent perspective. A few days later during a speech before the Senate, he said: 'Today every American shares the dreams, the thrills, the spirit and the memories of those incredible two weeks. Every American owns a share of stock in the accomplishments of those athletes. But in a very real sense, the victories, the excitement, the pure joy belongs to the nation. For one moment the nation was a family. The moment was ours.'

"I think we do ourselves an injustice, however, if we don't pause for a moment to review the ingredients that combined to create that Miracle on Ice. Those ingredients are not the sole property of the U.S. Hockey

THE ROAD TO GOLD		
USA, 2	—	Sweden, 2
USA, 7	—	Czechoslovakia, 3
USA, 5	—	Norway, 1
USA, 7	—	Romania, 2
USA, 4	—	West German, 2
USA, 4	—	Soviet Union, 3
USA, 4	—	Finland, 2

team, they are the foundation for any successful team or organization. Of course, you start with people. Teams are not brick and mortar, you have to have the right people. And good people aren't enough. I told our players at Lake Placid; 'Gentlemen, you do not have enough talent to win on talent alone...'.

"I believe that we as managers, parents and coaches must say at times things that employees, children and athletes do not want to hear. Things such as 'You do not have enough talent to win on talent alone.' That brings us to the hidden ingredients, the intangibles, the things you can't see, can't weigh, can't buy, can't sell, or can't put a price tag on.

"At our training camp in Colorado Springs, we began with talented young men. Our challenge as coaches was to break down the individual stereotypes into one cohesive unit working toward a common goal. Our players had to draw strength from association as a team. And they had to have the will to win. Practically every person has a will to win, but those young men had something more — they had a will to prepare to win. I told our players to come to practice with a lunch pail and hard hat and to come ready to work. And the kids responded. If the television cameras had followed each individual player on the ice, when he had the puck and when he was skating without it, you would have seen what I mean. We had young men doing the unsung things that have to be done in hockey: forechecking, backchecking — the things that are just plain hard work. Our players spent months getting their noses dirty before they could spend those few seconds on that Olympic platform receiving a gold medal.

"The Russians have a saying: *'Passes come from the heart, not from the stick,'* meaning in hockey that you pass the puck at the most opportune time. You don't become an individual star and just pass when you say 'Hey, that's all I can do, I can't do any more.'.

"I take great pride in the fact that hockey people said we played the Russian game better than the Russians. We beat them at their own game. The months of hard work put us in a winning situation and once we got there, we didn't panic. We stayed with the game plan. We danced with the one who brung us.

"There are a lot of guys who just want to be on the team. Once they slip on the uniform, or a white shirt, they are satisfied. They think they've got it made. But the true achievers are those who are determined that their team isn't going to finish second. I told the team before the Russian game: 'They are ripe to be beat; they are complacent; and they are taking us too lightly.' If the roles had been reversed, I would have told my team: 'Don't get smug and don't rest on your laurels. There's a bunch of young, hungry teams out there ready to show the world that it's their turn to be on top.'

"I don't care whether you are X-Y-Z computer company just starting out or you're an IBM sitting at the top, there's always going to be a young U.S. Hockey team waiting out there to knock you off your pedestal. The intangibles; the spirit of a team; the strength of association; the power we generate when we work as a unit: these, I firmly believe, are the ingredients that the U.S. Hockey team drew from this great nation.

"A Canadian newspaper columnist recently wrote, 'When the Americans were down they never quit working, and even when they were up they worked even harder.' That rich heritage was manifested magnificently for two weeks in Lake Placid by 20 young men who showed the world that our way of life, our system, our people; have indeed made us the greatest nation on earth."

CH. 9) SOMETIMES IT'S ALL RIGHT TO PACK UP AND HEAD FOR THE HILLS

After the dust had finally settled in the days and weeks following the Icy Miracle, Brooks was able to sit down and figure out his next career move. He had already resigned from the University of Minnesota and believe it or not, was officially unemployed. Offers were pouring in though, and Brooks wanted to wait for just the right opportunity to come along. So, he laid low and headed overseas to coach in the Swiss Alps for a season. It would be the perfect chance to reconnect with his family, as far away from the media spotlight as possible.

When the hoopla surrounding the Olympics eventually calmed down, Brooks was finally able to weigh his career options. He had already decided that he did not want to return to the University of Minnesota, feeling that he had already accomplished what he had set out to do there. So, he was ready for a new challenge; something that would keep him energized and excited about hockey and about life. There were several NHL teams which had contacted him about becoming their next head coach, but Brooks wanted to make sure that the situation was right for him.

Of all the potential offers that were coming in, one in particular stood out. You see, Brooks' longtime friend and former teammate, Craig Patrick, who was the general manager of the 1980 Olympic team, had just gotten hired to be the new GM of the NHL's New York Rangers. Patrick told Brooks that he wanted him to be his next head coach, but that there was a stipulation. He needed him to wait for one season because the current Rangers coach, Fred Shero, was in the last year of his contract and Patrick did not want to come in and fire the guy right away. So, he told Brooks to just lay low for a season and then the job would be his that next Summer.

With that, Brooks made the most of his unique situation and took a coaching position overseas in the Swiss pro league in Davos, Switzerland. There, he would be able to avoid the media spotlight and coach in an environment where there would be little pressure to 'win at

all costs.' He would also be able to rest and recharge his batteries too. So, the entire family packed up and headed for the hills, or Swiss Alps to be more precise, to embark on a new adventure.

Knowing that they were going to be gone for just one season, Herb decided to ask his friend, Craig Dahl, who was the head hockey coach at nearby Bethel College, to house-sit for him. Herbie used to joke that he wasn't worried about anything being missing when he got back either, because he figured anybody from a good Midwestern bible college was going to be about as honest and trustworthy as could be. It would be the beginning of a long and meaningful relationship between the two, and one that would pay dividends for Dahl down the road.

In Davos the Brooks family got reconnected. Herbie had been on the road traveling with the Olympic team for what had seemed like an eternity and this was just what the doctor ordered. They rented a villa on a golf course and embraced the new culture. It was about as far away from the limelight as he could get, and that was exactly what he needed.

The kids enrolled in a German speaking school and wound up having a ball. The family skated together; skied together and just hung out together. One of the unique things about the Swiss way of life was that the kids would come home from school to be with their families at lunch time. Even Herbie would leave the rink and come home from noon to two to spend some quality time with his wife and kids. It was something he had never done before, but certainly something he enjoyed.

Brooks' team played well in the Swiss League and things were going fine until he got into an argument with the team owner over his contract. They had some words and Herbie, who was very principled, decided that he had had enough. The team still had about a quarter of its season left, but Brooks didn't want to stick around. He was anxious to get back to the States so he could start preparing for his new job as the head coach of the New York Rangers.

With that, the family packed up and went home. There, they would be able to enjoy the Summer before packing up once again and moving to New York for their next big adventure. The nomadic lifestyle of a coach could be tough on a family, but luckily for Herbie his wife and kids embraced the situation and just went along for the ride.

Once he got home, Brooks began preparing a game plan for how he was going to guide the Rangers. The NHL was a whole new ball game for the coach, and he knew that he was going to have to come at it from a different angle in order to be successful. He was determined to go with a European style, however, which was going to be a radical change from anything which had ever been done before at that level.

Brooks even took over as the head coach of the U.S. National team that played in the world championships in Sweden that April, figuring it would be a good last minute tune-up in learning that particular style of play. From there, it was off to the Big Apple.

CH. 10) ADAPT & CHANGE OR GO BY WAY OF THE DINOSAUR; THE REWARDS FAR OUTWEIGH THE RISKS

As the Coach of the NHL's New York Rangers, Brooks revolutionized the game by introducing a radically different style of play. He took some big risks along the way, both on and off the ice, and was rewarded for his efforts. He also learned how to adapt as a head coach in an environment that was completely foreign to him. The motivational tactics which had worked so well on amateur players, had now become nearly obsolete. He would have to change his ways or risk failing. Of course, he would rise to the occasion.

As expected, Brooks accepted the head coaching position of the New York Rangers in June of 1981. The entire family made the trip as they once again packed up and moved, this time to Greenwich, Conn., just outside of New York City. It was a welcome homecoming back to the state of New York, where he had just made history in Lake Placid.

For Herbie, making the leap to the NHL, the pinnacle of professional hockey, was not going to be an easy transition. Many of Brooks' motivational tactics that worked on amateur players in the past were not going to fly with the big boys. So, he would have to change and adapt. He was up for the challenge though. He would introduce a European style of free-flowing offense to the "Blue Shirts," as they were affectionately known in Manhattan.

It didn't take long for Brooks to gel with his players and to get them to buy into his new system. Disciplined defense, crisp passes and speed were all hallmarks of the hybrid style, and the players liked it. With it, the smaller, quicker and more skilled position players could thrive, even against the bigger, tougher skaters. Remember, during this era the Rangers had to go up against some really tough teams, including Philadelphia, Boston and their cross-town rivals, the New York Islanders. Brooks used the players on his roster who he felt were the most conducive to thriving in his new system, and for the most part it was the smaller, quicker players who got the most ice time.

Before long the media had tabbed Brooks' Rangers as the

"Smurfs," in reference to the little blue guys from the popular cartoon series. Brooks didn't care what they called them, as long as his teams were winning. And they were. It soon became apparent that the way for other teams to try to beat the Rangers was to play rough. This worked out great because the smaller, faster skaters had no problem maneuvering around the bigger goons who were trying to slow them down.

And, even though Brooks' Rangers were designed for speed, they were still tough. That had always been a hallmark of his teams because he understood how important it was to be able to protect his top players from being intimidated. Arguably Brooks' favorite player in that capacity was Nick Fotiu, a grizzled veteran enforcer who grew up just across the Hudson River in Staten Island. Nicky was a huge fan favorite at the Garden, they loved him. He was a blue collar guy who wasn't afraid to do a lot of the dirty work that other players weren't interested in doing. Brooks could relate. He appreciated guys like that and and gave them opportunities. They hit it off from the start and would later even become close friends.

"He knew how to get players to buy into his philosophy," said Fotiu. "Then, he knew how to be creative. He just had the ability to get guys to believe, and I was one of those guys. I would have followed him anywhere. You had to work hard for Herb, but it usually paid off in the end. He didn't trust a lot of people either, so if you were in his circle, it was a real honor. He surrounded himself with the people he trusted the most and that was important to him. The guy was so determined, in whatever he did, and he was very honest. That was the secret to his success."

Brooks posted a 39-27-14 record during his freshman campaign in the NHL, good for 92 points and a second place finish in the tough Patrick Division. Led by 40-goal scorer Ron Duguay, the team then went on to beat Philadelphia's Broad Street Bullies three games to one in the opening round of the Stanley Cup Playoffs. Herbie could only smile as the Philly fans threw plastic Smurf figurines out onto the ice after the game in protest of his coaching style, which had worked masterfully against the bigger, slower Flyers. New York would then advance on to the Patrick Division Finals, only to get beat by the Islanders, a dynasty team which was in the midst of winning four straight Stanley Cups. The Rangers played inspired hockey though and for his efforts, Brooks earned Coach of the Year honors.

That next season, 1982-83, the team swept Philly in the opening round of the playoffs. With that they had advanced back to the Patrick Division Finals for the second straight time, only to get bounced out of the post-season yet again by the Islanders. Losing was something Brooks was not very good at. Sure, he was gracious in defeat, but instead of getting angry, he would analyze things until the wee hours of the morning. He would replay certain events in his mind, second guessing his decisions and outcomes, over and over.

Mark Pavelich, who played on the 1980 U.S. Olympic Team, later joined the Rangers and even scored 40 goals for the Blue Shirts one season. He remembered one incident in particular about Brooks' pension for losing and how it effected others.

"One of my friends who was a trainer at Madison Square Garden told me a funny story about Herbie one time," recalled Pavelich. "He said that after games, particularly when we lost, that Herbie used to mill around the locker room for a while. Eventually, the janitors would come in to clean the place up. Well, Herbie would have to vent his frustration at someone, so he would drag these guys in. Now, these guys knew absolutely nothing about hockey, but they would come in and Herbie would sit them down and he would break down plays on the chalk board for them to analyze at midnight. They would pretend like they were interested, but they just wanted him to shut up so they could finish their jobs and get home. A few of them didn't even speak English! So, after that, these guys would totally avoid him if the Rangers lost and hide until they saw him leave. When I heard that I just had to laugh, because that was so Herbie."

In 1984 Brooks was behind the bench for one of the franchise's greatest playoff series, the divisional semifinal against the Islanders. It was the team's third straight meeting with the Isles and after two straight losses, Brooks was anxious to finally get that monkey off of his back. After losing the opener, 4-1, at Nassau Coliseum, Brooks led his underdog Rangers to consecutive 3-0 and 7-2 victories over the Isles.

Then, just when things were looking up, a shoulder injury to their

top defenseman, Barry Beck, left a gaping hole in their blue line corps. As a result, they lost Game Four, 4-1, at the Garden, setting up the classic rubber match out in Uniondale, Long Island. Down 3-2 late in the third period, the Rangers rallied to tie and sent the game into overtime. There, the Rangers had at least three golden scoring chances, but were robbed by All-Star goalie Billy Smith each time. Ironically, it was Ken Morrow, one of Brooks' protégés from the 1980 gold medal team that notched the game-winner past a screened Glen Hanlon to give the Isles the series. It was a heart breaking loss for Brooks and for all of Manhattan.

Brooks felt that Beck, a potential All-Star, was an underachiever. So he rode him hard that next season, prodding him to play up to his potential. He allegedly even called him a "coward," a charge which Brooks later denied. It all came to a fiery climax during a practice session, however, and from there the press wouldn't leave it alone. It would cause a rift between the two and the problem only festered under the glare of the New York media jackals. Brooks' motivational tactics, which had worked brilliantly on the college and Olympic players, weren't going to fly with temperamental and arrogant millionaire players who yielded a lot of clout with management.

So, three quarters of the way through that next season, Brooks decided that he had had enough. It had been a long four years on Broadway and he was ready to try his hand at something new. He had just gotten tired of dealing with players who didn't show him the same respect that he had been accustomed to, and he wanted out. He was also frustrated with the team's lack of personnel moves. In college, if he needed a quick centerman or a stay-at-home defenseman, he would either recruit one or call one up from the Junior ranks. In the NHL, however, it was much more difficult to get management to make a deal for the type of players that he wanted. There were contract issues and

ON LEADERS & LEADERSHIP...

"I don't know if there is any one real definition of a leader. Leadership is not a function of titles but of relationships. You have to wear a lot of different hats as a leader. There is a time to talk and a time to listen, and a good leader knows this. Leadership is a much debated topic. Leaders are visionaries. Leaders are not managers. Leaders give people something to believe in, then they've got something to belong to and then they have something to follow. That is a real key component of a good leader. Most importantly, leadership is the battle for the hearts and minds of others. It is not a spectator sport and it is not necessarily a popularity contest either. Leaders have to show good habits and have to display a sincere purpose and passion for what they are doing." — *Herb Brooks* trading deadlines to contend with, and it was out of his control. Brooks was also sick and tired of living in hotel rooms away from his family, who had moved back to Minnesota the year before. Couple that with the fact that his father had died during training camp that season, and the writing was on the wall. It was time to move on. The media would say he was fired, but those who were 'in the know,' knew better. Herbie's friend and boss, Craig Patrick, reluctantly agreed and they parted ways.

In the professional ranks, Brooks did things which were truly revolutionary at the time. He had off-season training back when off-season training consisted of golf and fishing. He brought in his old friend from Minnesota, Jack Blatherwick, to teach his players about exercise physiology, and it payed off. He monitored his players' body fat and insisted that they eat right, and even chew sugar free gum. Then, he instilled a wide open style of hockey into the rough and tumble, clutch and grab, dump and chase North American game which had been commonplace for decades. People thought he was crazy, but when his Smurfs nearly upset the Stanley Cup champion Islanders in back to back seasons, no one was laughing. Herb truly changed the game and proved that he could coach with great success at the NHL level.

In all, Brooks posted a very respectable 131-113-41 overall regular season record with the Rangers, good for a .532 winning percentage. He also earned 100 victories faster than any other Ranger coach before him in team history. In addition, he garnered a 12-12 post-season record with the franchise as well. Not bad for a guy who was coaching bantams just a decade earlier.

Herb's son Dan had a very unique perspective on his dad's time in New York. The two spent a lot of time together out there, driving to and from games, and on team trips. In his own words, Dan provides some insight into the events which ultimately led to his father's decision to step down as the head coach of the Rangers. He also provides some very poignant family background history about his father and his grandfather as well.

"My dad finally decided to leave New York because he just got sick of it," said Dan. "We were all back in Minnesota and the grind of it all eventually got to him. He was tired of the media and tired of dealing with millionaire players who didn't want to listen to him. Plus, his dad had recently died and that was probably the final straw that pushed him over the edge.

"My grandfather, Herb Sr., was a huge fan and supporter of my dad. They had an interesting relationship. They were friends, but I wouldn't say that they were really close or anything. They had a lot of respect for one another though. My grandfather was a recovered alcoholic and there was always some tension because of that. I don't want to say that he had any inner demons or anything, but it had an effect on him in a way that I will never fully understand. As a result, my dad was a little bit stand-offish around him. My grandfather wasn't a mean drunk or anything like that, he just liked to hang out with his east side buddies at the bar a lot. He was a great guy though, somebody who was always the life of the party. Everyone loved him. He eventually went through treatment back in the early '70s and got cleaned up. I actually spent more time with my grandfather than anybody, and I was very close with him.

"I will never forget, he died on the golf course in October of 1984. My dad had just left for training camp. Two weeks prior to him leaving, we all played a round of golf together over at Goodrich Golf Course, not too far from Aldrich Arena. My dad was begging my grandfather to let him buy him a cart to drive. My grandfather, meanwhile, was very stubborn and insisted on walking. So, fast-forward to a few weeks later when my dad was off at training camp, and my grandfather was out golfing. He is on the 17th hole, hits his tee shot, walks 50 yards towards his ball, and then falls over and dies of a massive heart attack right there on the fairway.

"My dad flew home for the funeral and was a wreck. I can still remember trying to fall asleep up in my bedroom and hearing him crying downstairs because he was so upset and distraught over the fact that he hadn't been able to tell his father that he loved him. It was very, very hard on him. Even though my grandfather knew, my dad just never told him that. So, from that point on, my dad really wasn't ever the same.

"A few years later I remember being home from college and was packing up to leave for the long drive back out to school at Denver University. It was around five o'clock in the morning and I wanted to get an early start out on the road. I remember it was pouring rain outside as I was getting my car and U-Haul all packed up. Well, my dad was up and like a mad-man, he was just following me around the house. I mean he was literally right on my heals as I was running around and trying to get packed up to leave.

"Finally, I was all ready to go and I made a mad dash out to my car so I wouldn't get soaking wet. Sure enough, my dad is still right on my heals. As I run to my car, he grabs my shoulder, turns me around and looks right at me. I mean there is like a five second pause as we are standing there in the rain, and it seemed like 15 minutes. He looked me right in the eye, took a deep breath, and said 'I love you.' Then, he ran back into the house. That was it. Not a day goes by in my life where I don't see that image of the rain pouring down and hearing those words from my father. I think I cried the whole way to Colorado. I knew what was going through his mind and knew that he did not want to make the same mistake of not telling me that he loved me like he had done to his father. That haunted him. I will remember that for the rest of my life."

CH. 11) GIVING BACK IS ABOUT MORE THAN JUST MONEY, AND CAN BE EXTREMELY GRATIFYING

After leaving New York, Brooks had gained a lot of political clout in the hockey world. Instead of cashing it in on another high paying head coaching position in the NHL though, he chose instead to do what he felt was the right thing. He followed his heart to tiny St. Cloud State University, where, under the urging of his mentor, John Mariucci, he took the program from Division III to Division I status. This move would be all about getting more Minnesota kids more opportunities to play college hockey. It was also about growing the base of the pyramid, a cause that was near and dear to Herbie's heart.

When Herb came home to Minnesota he took some time off to recharge his batteries. One of the things he enjoyed during that time was being more involved with his Summer hockey camps, "Minnesota Hockey Schools," which he ran with long-time friend Chuck Grillo. He made a few bucks; had a good time teaching kids the fundamentals; and loved hanging around his former players and coaches who came out to work with him. The camp, which started in the early '80s, was originally head-quartered down in Faribault, at Shattuck, and later moved up to Brainerd. Herbie was a huge fan and supporter of youth hockey, and his camps were considered among the very best in the business with regards to teaching kids the right way to play the game.

Before long Brooks got the itch to coach again. There had been much speculation as to where he would wind up following his successful tenure in New York. Other NHL teams had inquired about hiring his services, but the coach this time decided to follow his heart rather than his wallet. He followed it straight up Interstate 94 West and right into the heart of St. Cloud, Minn. There, under the urging of his former coach and mentor, John Mariucci, Brooks accepted the head coaching position at St. Cloud State University. It was a no-frills gig, but one that meant a great deal to him nonetheless. His mission was to guide the team for the 1986-87 season and put them on the hockey map.

He had one condition, that he be allowed to hand pick his top assistant, Craig Dahl, who he would personally groom to take over the head coaching duties when he left. They agreed. Dahl, of course, had a long history with Brooks and even house-sat for him while he was living in both Switzerland and New York. Together, they would build the program from the ground up and have a ball in the process. When it was all said and done, Brooks would be revered as the school's savior, leading the Huskies to a 25-10-1 record; a third place finish in the national

Herbie with his mentor, John Mariucci

small-college tournament; and more importantly, getting the program elevated from Division III to Division I status. He stayed for only a year, but with his clout, he was able to lobby the state legislature and get the school a beautiful new arena, The National Sports Center.

"It was a wonderful experience," said Brooks. "The President of St. Cloud State, Dr. McDonald, along with Bill Radovich, a St. Cloud State Vice President, Morris Kurtz, the Athletic Director, various members of the administration, and many people in the St. Cloud community, wanted to have a Division One hockey program. We sold the concept to the state legislature, the governor, and the people of Central Minnesota, raised $10 million dollars, built the arena and somehow got it done. Look at them now, it's a great, great story."

Brooks went to St. Cloud as a personal favor to John Mariucci, who had reminded him about the importance of giving back to the community. Brooks wanted to build the base of the pyramid and get more Minnesota kids opportunities to play college hockey. It would prove to be one of the most satisfying years of his life.

"I look back and think about my father, who started one of the very first youth hockey associations in the state of Minnesota," recalled Brooks. "From that I saw the spirit of volunteerism on a first hand basis and think it is a very powerful and tremendous thing. Now, moving on, I saw that same spirit when I was coaching at the University of Minnesota. One of my mentors was John Mariucci, who told me that I was more than just a coach and that I needed to reach out and help the growth of the game throughout the state. I have always remembered that and as a result have always tried to do as much as I could to help the coaches, administrators and volunteers to grow the game. He said it was not about what you accomplish, but what you really contribute towards. He gave countless hours of his time to youth hockey associations through whatever means he could to promote the game. I just tried to follow his lead. You know, it was really one of the best things I have ever done in hockey. I made only $15,000 that season, but would do it all over again in a heartbeat. It was a real labor of love and that's what it's all about — giving back to the game."

Dahl couldn't have been more pleased. Brooks had brought him along for the ride of his life and then handed him the keys. Brooks knew that he needed a good man to take the ball and run with it from there and that is exactly what Dahl would do over the ensuing years.

"I remember when we were lobbying for our new arena," recalled Dahl. "Herbie stayed up at my apartment one night after we were out working all day and I got a phone call at about 6:30 in the morning from the president of the university. He asked for Herb, so I gave him the phone. Herb gets up right away and starts talking. A few minutes later he hangs up and says, ' I gotta get dressed right away because the legislature is having their final push this morning with the speaker of the house and the head of appropriations.' So, he got up and took off. He came back later that day and said, 'We're going to get our arena.' Sure enough, he helped to push it through and we got our new arena. I can't imagine where the program would be today without it. That was Herbie, he had a lot of clout and could just get things done."

Herb's legacy in the Granite City would include many things, among them being the success of one of the program's first stars, Bret Hedican. Hedican, who played for the Huskies from 1990-91, went on to become an NHL All-Star defenseman and 2006 Stanley Cup Champion. The North St. Paul native would also later play for Brooks as a member of the 2002 Olympic team.

"You know, the only time I really spent any time with Herbie was at the 2002 Olympic pre-camp try-outs, but what he means to me is immeasurable," he said. "I don't think that I would have had the opportunities that I have had over my career without him. I mean, he put St. Cloud State Hockey on the map, and that is where I got my start. I had one scholarship offer out of high school and that was at St. Cloud, so without that I don't know where I would be. If it hadn't have been for him going up there and turning that program into a Division One school, who knows what would have happened. Herb was committed to having more kids playing hockey in Minnesota and I was a direct result of that vision. So, I thank him every time I lace em' up, because where I am today was a direct result of his efforts back then. I was a St. Paul guy and he was a St. Paul guy and I think we had that connection too. He was a great person and someone that I really looked up to and respected."

Another situation that was going on at the home front during this

time was the fact that Herbie's son, Dan, was about to make a decision with regards to which college he was going to attend. Dan had emerged as an outstanding prep player at St. Thomas Academy and had gotten scholarship offers from a handful of Division I schools. The one school that Dan was most interested in, however, was the University of Minnesota, where he grew up watching his father's Gophers. The problem was that Gopher Coach Doug Woog had not directly made him an offer to play there.

This was going to be a touchy subject for Herbie, who had lobbied to get Woog that job a few years earlier, and was probably expecting a little different response. He did not want to get involved politically though and stayed out of it. As a result, Dan respectfully looked elsewhere and wound up getting a full-ride from the University of Denver instead.

When Dan graduated from DU four years later, he had several options. One of which was to sign with the NHL's St. Louis Blues, which had owned his draft rights. He was burned out of hockey by that point though and opted instead to begin his career in the financial world. He had already cashed his signing bonus though and needed to do what he felt was the right thing.

So, he drove to St. Louis and personally thanked the team's general manager for the opportunity. He then returned the signing bonus money, all $30 grand of it. That was a lot of money for a kid straight out of college, but something he just felt strongly about.

Undoubtedly, Herbie was torn. On one hand he must have certainly been extremely proud that his son had done such an honorable thing, when he clearly did not have to. On the other hand, however, he must have been devastated that his only son had decided to walk away from the game he so dearly loved. Without a doubt, a little bit of his dream, to have his son play in the NHL, died that day too.

ON GOALS...

"The joy, fulfillment and self satisfaction you receive when you accomplish another challenging goal is beyond description. It's the ecstasy of sport. But the agony is just as real. You will, and probably already have, experienced considerable frustrations and disappointment and doubt. The key is to know and understand that it's coming. That it's a necessary part of the progress. Don't run from it. Attack it . Fight it. Regroup, and shortly you'll break through, only to find yourself ever closer to achieving your goal.

"You must have goals in your life, or otherwise be prepared to be used by those people who do have them. Where there are no goals, neither will their ever be significant accomplishments, only existence. Do you just want to exist?"   — *Herb Brooks*

ON DISCIPLINE...

"Have you ever wondered why certain people almost always succeed at whatever they do? High achievers seem to have a talent for thinking big. They have a sixth sense for knowing when and how to develop their ideas, and a driving ambition that gives them the confidence to do the right thing at the right time. How do these people achieve so much even though they appear to start with so little? The answer is simple, they are disciplined.

"On the long, hard road to success, there is one characteristic alone that will determine whether you ever reach your goal. It is not intelligence. It is not talent. It is not luck. And it is not "who you know." It is plain old fashion discipline, but with a new modern day meaning — a meaning from locker rooms, board rooms, class rooms, and family rooms.

"But before I get into that definition, be assured that all the brains, inspiration and education in the world won't get you past the starting gate of achievement and self-fulfillment. With it, there is truly no goal that is out of reach. Because self-discipline keeps you on the path to success no matter how long it takes or what obstacles may be thrown in your way.

"In our quick fix society that aims for immediate gratification, many people think self discipline means suffering and self denial. Today, too many are looking for that short cut in life. Yes we have become a quick fix society, a "now" society. I want it now, what I see on TV because tomorrow is too late. If it feels good, I'll try it, relief is just a swallow away. Temptation resisted is the true measure of character.

"Yet nothing could be further from the truth. Self discipline is what enables you to achieve life-long gratification through the rewards that come from the patient planning and realization of your most cherished goals. Though many people seem born with an iron will, self discipline is not an inherited trait. One sees it, learns it, witnesses it and feels it. Without a doubt it is the essential factor that lifts one man above his fellows in terms of achievement and success. It is his greatest capacity for self discipline."

— Herb Brooks

CH. 12) MAKE THE MOST OF BAD SITUATIONS; LOSE THE BATTLE BUT WIN THE WAR

After leaving St. Cloud, Brooks returned to the NHL, only this time with his hometown Minnesota North Stars. He was thrilled to be back in the big leagues and was determined to make the most of his opportunity. What transpired, however, was nothing short of a disaster. Injuries plagued the team's top players and midway through the season a new general manager was brought in to shake things up. Brooks did what he could with what he had, but eventually decided to walk away on his own terms. He knew that there would be other coaching positions to come, in much better circumstances. It would be a tough lesson in "losing the battle but winning the war."

After leaving St. Cloud State University, Herbie was anxious to get back into the NHL. So, when the hometown North Stars came calling, he jumped at the opportunity. Herbie's longtime friend and former teammate, Lou Nanne, was the team's general manager at the time and was excited about the opportunity for Brooks to take over behind the bench. He would be the first native Minnesotan to coach the team.

Brooks had originally turned down an offer to become the head coach of the team back in 1978, because he had insisted upon getting a three-year contract, which they weren't willing to do. So, he said no thanks. This time around, however, he felt that the timing was right. He wound up signing a two-year deal and was ready for the challenge of turning the franchise around. The added pressure of being the home town coach was there, but Brooks was determined not to let it be a distraction. He knew most of the members of the media and relished the chance to finally have them in his corner, unlike the situation he had just come from in New York.

The task at hand was not going to be easy. The team had missed the playoffs for the first time in seven years that previous season and wound up finishing in the Norris Division cellar. They were in desperate need of some new blood and were hoping that Brooks would be the answer. What ultimately happened that season, however, was nothing short of a disaster. Nearly every star player on the team was on the shelf

at one point or another with an injury and the team wound up finishing in last place with a league-worst 19-48-13 record. It would prove to be one of Brooks' most trying times as a professional.

Brooks worked hard though and demanded that the players who were healthy enough to suit up, give their best effort. His players weren't immune from his mind tricks either, especially when they weren't playing up to their abilities.

"I remember walking down the corridor at the Met Center past the locker room and towards the ice for the start of a game," recalled Stars winger Brian Lawton. "Well, as I got there I saw Herbie waiting for me. 'Lawton,' he says, 'get over here!' So he grabbed me and pulled me aside pretty firmly by the arm and said to me 'if you don't score tonight I am going to have to trade you.' That was it. That was all he said. And he was dead serious too. Well, luckily for me, because I hadn't been playing very well at the time, I scored on like my third shift of the game when a slapshot deflected, literally, off of my ass and into the side of the net. It was not a pretty goal by any stretch, but I was elated. I remember skating over to the ref and telling him that the puck definitely hit me and to make sure that I got credit for the goal. So, I headed back to the bench and told Herb that I tallied that one just for him. He just looked at me and said, 'you're pretty damn lucky Lawton...'. You know, we used to laugh about that whenever I saw him. He had some strange ways of motivating guys, but that one took the cake for me."

The season turned out to be a catastrophe for Brooks as he was constantly forced to improvise and juggle his lines, resulting in very little continuity with his players. To make matters even worse, his biggest ally, Lou Nanne, wound up resigning midway through the year as the team's general manager and was replaced by Jack Ferreira.

Ferreira and Brooks had issues from the get-go and didn't see eye to eye on how the team should be run. It was only a matter of time before something had to give. Again, the writing was on the wall. Citing "philosophical differences with management," Brooks ultimately wound up resigning after the season. Herbie knew that he would coach again, but felt strongly that this particular situation was not conducive for him to thrive in. So, he left on his own terms.

"The North Stars year was tough," Brooks would later recall. "The funny thing is, you learn the true meaning of persistence, comradeship, principles and ethics under those circumstances. I've probably got more motivational stories from the North Stars year than from the Olympics year. In 1980 it was easy for me to take bows with people saying, 'What persistence, what determination!' But you only learn the real meanings of human relationships when it's low-down and dirty and there's not a lot of bells and whistles."

Here is how Herb's son, Dan, remembers that season: "That was a tough time for my dad," recalled Dan. "It was a total disaster year for him. They didn't have any defensemen or any goaltending, and it seemed like the entire team was injured. Neal Broten and Craig Hartsburg were on the shelf and Dino Cicarelli had gotten into trouble for running around his house naked, which was a huge distraction in the media. Even Louie Nanne, who was the GM at the time, quit at mid-season to boot. The entire thing just fell apart from the beginning.

"I think he could have gone back to coach again that next season, but he was so pissed off about the guy they hired to replace Louie as the new GM, Jack Ferreira, that he said 'screw it.' My dad couldn't stand him. He felt that he didn't treat the scouts with the respect that they deserved and didn't want anything to do with him. Apparently, he had sent a letter to the team's scouting department and in it, he wrote 'Henry Howell' instead of 'Harry Howell,' who was an NHL Hall of Famer and a guy my dad had a great deal of respect for. Now, with all due respect to Jack, I am sure it was probably just a typo, but my dad went ballistic. My dad always stuck up for the little guy and was so insulted that Jack would show such disrespect.

"Dad took it personally and went after Jack. He pissed him off to the point where Jack basically said, 'screw you, we will hire someone else to be our coach.' My dad probably had an ulterior motive for getting fired, I don't know. But he loved the battles and was just so principled in what he felt was right. When he got upset over something, there were going to be problems. I think it was the east side blue collarness in him to tell you the truth. For whatever the reason, he wasn't about to let the scouts, the underpaid behind-the-scenes guys, get screwed over. So, he burned any bridges that may have allowed him to coach again that

ON GETTING OUT OF A SLUMP...

"As coaches we know the importance of dreaming of long term and short term goals. But despite everything from all aspects of training, slumps do occur. If you remember to attack slumps right away by not letting them linger, you'll be better off. You will need to lead by example. Know your players and know which ones to pat and which ones to kick. There is a big difference. Slumps will eventually work themselves out, but there are tools to deal with them. Begin by realizing that players have lost their confidence. There may be too much tension, bad attitudes and rationalization.

"So, start fresh with new expectations, new outlooks and new perspectives. First, get the players to admit the slump is from questionable attitudes and beliefs. Second, take a day off; third, have fun in your training sessions or work-outs; fourth, work physically harder to start building confidence, but be ready to compliment your players; and fifth, try to eliminate any pressures that may be causing the situation. Lastly, work like crazy to get a win. Winning solves most of these problems. Also, try to maintain the group setting, because the peer group pressure will ensure that nobody will want to let anybody else down."
— *Herb Brooks*

next season.

"Regardless of what was written, he left the organization on his own terms. They brought in Pierre Page that next year and my dad was just relieved to be out of that situation. It was extremely hard for him though. It was his big homecoming, getting to coach in Minnesota again, and it definitely did not go the way he had envisioned."

Former North Star player J.P. Parise served as assistant coach under Brooks that season and remembered it this way: "I never really got to know Herbie until I started to work with him that year," recalled Parise. "It was one of the most wonderful years of my life, being with him. I remember even after our first practice with the team, I came to my desk that next day and he had left me a nice note which read: 'Great start Jeeper, let's keep it going!' That meant so much to me. He gave me a lot of responsibilities with the team and treated me with nothing but class. He gave me advice not only about hockey, but about life. He was very astute and very smart. He really made my life better and cared so much about me. He was just a wonderful human being."

All in all, Brooks was able to learn a lot from his otherwise forgettable experience with the Stars, especially the virtues of the old saying: "lose the battle but win the war." Brooks dealt with a lot of adversity in that situation and ultimately knew when to get out and cut his losses. He also learned a lot about making the most of a bad situation. As a coach, it was extremely difficult to deal with injuries and other situations which were out of his control. He would move on and learn from the entire ordeal, making him a stronger coach and person in the long run.

CH. 13) TAKE TIME OFF TO REGROUP, AND THEN COME BACK REINVIGORATED

Brooks would take some much needed time off after his brief stint with the North Stars. During that time he regrouped and refocused his career goals. He got away from coaching for a while and worked with several local companies in a variety of capacities. Brooks wasn't too proud to take a job in the real world. In fact, he enjoyed it. It gave him a different perspective on life, which would later prove invaluable for when he was able to return to his post behind the bench — this time with the New Jersey Devils.

Following the North Stars debacle, Brooks took the next two years off from coaching. He stayed plenty busy though. In addition to working as a motivational speaker, he also served as a color commentator for Sports Channel America NHL telecasts. He would later describe that feeling of broadcasting hockey games like "being a recovering alcoholic and having to work in a bar...", explaining just how much he missed being behind the bench at games. Brooks even took a few day-jobs over the years to keep busy. He had previously worked with Twin Cities-based Jostens Inc., selling national prestige awards to high end clients such as the NFL and NBA, a few years earlier, and enjoyed it very much. So, he signed on to do some promotional work with 3M that year. He also worked for Turnquist Paper for a short while and later served as a consultant with The St. Paul Companies as well.

Despite the fact that he had achieved fame and fortune, Brooks was not too proud to get a "real" job and earn an honest living for his family. Heck, he really liked it. He enjoyed new challenges and found the work to be interesting. Plus, he was always able to then use that insight from those real life experiences to apply back to his real passion, coaching hockey.

It is interesting to note that Herb had actually lobbied USA Hockey during this time to become the coach of the 1992 U.S. Olympic team. He knew that was an environment where he could make a difference with young people and he wanted to rebuild the U.S. program, which had fallen in recent years. So, he proposed the development of a full-time U.S. National team, made up of non-NHL players which would stay together after competing in the 1992 Winter Games in Albertville, France, and then compete again at the 1994 Winter Games in Lillehammer, Norway.

The powers-that-be at USA Hockey loved the idea, but were only willing to hire him for the 1992 Games. They wanted to see how it worked out before they promised him the 1994 campaign as well. It was a unique situation right then, in that the Summer and Winter Olympics were going to start alternating every two years, instead of four, starting in 1994. This presented an ideal opportunity in Brooks' eyes, to build continuity with the same team over that two to three year period, much like the other international teams do. But, when they balked at his idea, Herb, very principled, just walked away.

Brooks took the time to watch and analyze a lot of hockey during this time as well, which allowed him to keep his head in the game. He loved all aspects of the sport and knew that he could have an impact at a variety of different coaching and player personnel positions. In fact, back in July of 1989, the New York Rangers had offered him the team's general manager position, but he stalled over contractual issues and eventually lost out to Neil Smith.

He did eventually wind up taking a job in New York though, only this one was a few years later as the head coach of the Utica Devils, the New Jersey Devils' top minor league team based out of Utica, NY, in the American Hockey League. The year was 1991 and Brooks was ready to

A SPEECH TO
STUDENT-ATHLETES...

"Let me start with issuing you a challenge: Be better than you are; set a goal that seems unattainable; and when you reach that goal, set another one even higher.

"Let me first try to tell you 'Why you?' Because, my young friends, you are a select group, selected for physical prowess and tempered through hours of sweat and tears, and of wins and losses. You have exposed yourselves to the greatest laboratory of character available to young men and women of our nation in this day and age. For athletics teaches you: to be proud and unbending in honest failure; humble and gentle in success; not to substitute words for actions; not to seek the path of comfort, but to face the stress and spur of difficulty and challenge; to learn to stand up in the storm but to also have compassion for those who fall; to master yourself before you seek to master others; to have a heart that is clean; a goal that is high; to learn to laugh, yet never forget how to weep; to reach into the future, yet never neglect the past; to be serious, yet never to take yourself too seriously; to be captivated by an idea; to lose yourself in something bigger than you are; to be modest so that you will remember the simplicity of true greatness, the open mind of true wisdom, the meekness of true strength.

"For the cowards never started, and the weak died on the way." Because you are thus equipped, you have an obligation to your family, your school, yourself, your nation, and your god. An obligation that demands you take these lessons you have learned so dearly, and expand upon them. As William James once said, 'The great use of life is to spend it for something that outlasts it.' And, as Green Bay Packers Coach Vince Lombardi once said, 'Each man, whatever the degree of talent bestowed upon him, has a moral obligation, not only to himself but to society, to develop that gift to its utmost.'

"The only thing that makes you different from an animal is the fact that you are capable of dreaming dreams and seeing visions and following through to make them come true for something besides the selfish. Every one of you here is either part of the problem, or part of the answer as far as our nation is concerned. And now you say to me, 'All right, coach, I want to be part of the answer, what can I do?' What can you do? You can accept my original challenge: Be better than you are; set a goal that seems unattainable; and when you reach that goal, set another one even higher.

"You now face a new world. A world of change. The thrust into outer space of the satellite, spheres, and missiles marks a beginning of another epoch in the long story of mankind. We're faced with a world that will require courage, determination, a fighting spirit and inspiration. These glowing objectives that once depicted the wonders of the All-American boy may now well become a requirement for survival.

"Since the beginning of the history of man, 19 of 21 great civilizations have risen and died. They have all followed the same path. First, people in bondage, then a rise to spiritual faith. Then courage, liberty and abundance. Then to selfishness, to complacency, to apathy, to dependence and back again to bondage.

"In an effort to solve the problems of yourself, your community, and your nation — by your very presence here tonight, you possess the greatest of all admirable character traits - courage. What is courage? Let me tell you what I think it is. An indefinable quality that makes a man put out that extra something, when it seems there is nothing else to give. Ladies and gentlemen, I dare you to be better than you are. I dare you to be a thoroughbred. I might best describe this by telling you a story about the courage of a man taken from the Bible: the story of Eleazar.

"Let me refer to a story in the Old Testament, a story a lot of you have never heard. It is not about Goliath. It is about a young captain in King David's army. His name was Eleazar. One day King David called his captains together and said, "We have lost most every day to the Philistines and unless we win tomorrow, you come to the point of no return. Unless we win tomorrow, as a nation, we are sunk." He said, "Is there anyone that can lead us to victory?"

"And one man spoke up and said, 'There is a young captain named Eleazar. He hasn't had much experience, but he seems to have what it takes.' "Send for him.' He was called in and King David told him the situation, how they were at the end of their rope and how he was chosen to lead the forces tomorrow. He said, 'Well, I want 10,000 men, and equip them as best we can.' They then went out that next morning to do battle against the Philistines.

"But the Philistines were giant-like, awesome people, and when they came face to face with them, some of Eleazar's men dropped their swords and retreated ungloriously. But the Bible says in the 23rd chapter of second Samuel that Eleazar and a few of his men fought so valiantly for the Lord God Jehovah, that they won a great victory that day.

"The story then ends with this sentence: "his hand clave unto the sword.' Because after the battle was over, if you read between the lines, he threw himself down on the ground almost totally exhausted. His lieutenants came up and they tried to get the sword loose from his hand, but he had gripped it so tightly that they couldn't get the fingers off, and they had to go down to the brook and get water. They bathed the back of his hand, loosened the muscles and pulled the fingers off one by one. Then they found that he had gripped the sword so tightly that the hilt of the sword had eaten into his hand. It was a bloody mess, and the story ends, "his hand clave unto the sword.'

"Remember, Eleazar won his great victory for two main reasons. First of all, because he took the sword with a tight grip. Nothing half-hearted, but with vigor and dedication of purpose. Lord, deliver me from the namby pamby kind of people who do things half way. Second, because he lost himself in something bigger than he was, he didn't know the sword was biting into his hand.

"He was too busy doing battle. He was too busy fighting for the team. You know, all of us are walking 24 hours a day, 365 days a year toward a little plot of ground. I'm walking toward it; nothing is stopping me. And I don't want a very fancy marker, but do you know what I'd really like to be worthy of? A small stone with the words upon it, 'His hand clave unto the sword.'

"The Lord didn't create each of us alike: Some are bigger. Some faster. Some taller. Some even a different color. But, my friends, we all can have dreams and desires. How about you? Would a little extra effort on your part bring up your grade point average? Would you have a better chance to make the team if you stayed after practice and worked on your blocking?

"Let me tell you something about yourselves. You are taller and heavier than any past generation in this country. You are spending more money, enjoying more freedom and driving more cars than ever before. Yet many of you are very unhappy. Some of you have never known the satisfaction of doing your best for the team; the joy of excelling in class; the wonderful feeling of completing a job—any job—and looking back on it knowing that you have done your best.

"I dare you to have your hair cut and not wilt under the comments of your so-called friends. I dare you to clean up your language. I dare you to honor your mother and father. I dare you to stand with your hand over your heart and sing the National Anthem so all can hear. I dare you to go to church without having to be compelled to go by your parents. I dare you to unselfishly help someone less fortunate than yourself and enjoy the wonderful feeling that goes with it. I dare you to become physically fit. I dare you to read a book that is not required in school. I dare you to look up at the stars, not down at the mud, and set your sights on one of them that until now you thought was unattainable. I dare you to be better than you are. I dare you to 'clave unto the sword.' I dare you to be a thoroughbred."

> "We come into this life all naked and bare;
> We go through this life with worry and care;
> We go from this life, We know not where;
> But if you're a thoroughbred here;
> You'll be a thoroughbred there."

"You can preach a better sermon with your lives than with your mouths."

— Herb Brooks

get back into the saddle. New Jersey was an up and coming team and he knew that if he did well for a season down in the minors, then the NHL bench job would be his.

He wound up guiding Utica to a 34-40-6 overall record that season, including a trip to the playoffs, a place the team had not been the previous year. It was a challenging time for him to be sure. Going down to the minors, after coaching in the NHL, was an adjustment. Buses replaced airplanes and Best Westerns replaced Hiltons. But, he knew that he was working towards something bigger, and sure enough, that next year he got the call to take over as the New Jersey Devil's head coach. After five years off, Herbie was back in the "show."

Brooks was thrilled to be back in the NHL for the 1992-93 season and was again determined to make the most of his opportunity. He enjoyed being back behind the bench and the players were receptive to his coaching style. The team played solid, fundamental hockey and were poised to make a post-season run in the playoffs. But, as was the case in other past situations, Herbie wound up bucking heads with the management early and often. The general manager there was Lou Lamoriello, a no-nonsense hockey man who liked to do things his own way. The two didn't see eye to eye on a lot of matters, especially with player personnel, and before you knew it, the writing was on the wall yet again. In particular, Brooks had some issues with one of the team's star players, Claude Lemieux, who proved to be a big distraction from the start.

In the end, Brooks would guide the Devils for what turned out to be one season, compiling a very respectable 40-37-7 record along the way. They would finish in fourth place in the rugged Patrick Division and wind up losing in the first round of the Stanley Cup Playoffs to the Pittsburgh Penguins in five games.

Here is how Herb's son, Dan, remembers that season: "New Jersey was another tough situation for my father because their GM, Lou Lamoriello, liked to change his coaches all the time," he said. "That guy felt that the head coach of the team was about as important as the equipment manager I think. For him it was all about letting the players do their thing and he didn't want anybody getting in their way. The coach, meanwhile, was just a guy behind the bench directing traffic as far as he was concerned. It was crazy. My dad wasn't into that at all, and wound up bucking heads there as well."

"Plus, to make that situation worse, my dad had to deal with Claude Lemieux, who he just couldn't stand. Lemieux was a good player, but a real cancer for the team; just very disruptive to the coaching staff. I mean not only did his opponents loathe the guy, but his own linemates couldn't stand him either. My dad wanted to trade him, but Lamoriello liked him.

"Team chemistry was an important component in my dad's coaching philosophy and if he couldn't control that, it was not going to work. He needed who he felt were the *right* players to be able to buy into his system. So, my dad decided to not go back that next season and he quit. He was so principled that he didn't care about the money or anything else. That is why I think my dad struggled as a coach in the NHL compared to the success he had in college and in the Olympics. Maybe he wasn't selfish enough? I don't know. A guy like Lemieux would have gotten cut long before he could have ever tampered with the team chemistry in any other environment he coached in though, that is for sure. In the NHL, however, player personnel was not his job, it was the general manager's.

"Coaching in the NHL was sort of like a drug for my dad I think. It was the pinnacle of hockey, the top, the peak. There was big money, fame and fortune, the whole nine yards. It was the ultimate competition amongst the best players and coaches in the world and that is what intrigued him about it so much. He wasn't in it for the money or the notoriety though, he could have cared less about that stuff. He wanted to challenge himself and he wanted to win. That was it. But, like any drug, there are side effects, and eventually the high wears off to the point where you realize that it just isn't that much fun. The hangover was, at times, more miserable than the joy of winning. So, he came home on his own terms."

Warren Strelow, who served as an assistant coach under Brooks in both New York and New Jersey, had his own unique perspective on how things changed for his old friend when he made the jump from the amateur to the professional ranks.

"Herb was great with the college and Olympic kids, but when he got into the pros it was different," recalled Strelow. "I think that even though he didn't have as much success in the pros than he did elsewhere, he was still a very good pro coach. He did have that one year in New York where they scored close to 100 points and then lost to the Islanders in seven games. But, I think if Herb could have been the coach, as well as the general manager or director of player personnel, he would still be coaching in the NHL right now. I mean in college he could go out and get the players who he wanted, but in the pros the players were assigned to him. So, if he would have been able to sign guys and trade for guys to get just the right mix that he wanted, he would have won a whole bunch of Stanley Cups."

"Even in New Jersey, he complained and complained about his centermen. He just thought that they couldn't compete with the centers that he had. I was with him as an assistant and I heard this from him all the time. I mean our number one guy would be number four anywhere else. We just did not have good centermen at the time. Well, he leaves that next year and wouldn't you know it, management changes everything and brings in some different centermen and they win the Stanley Cup.

"Conviction, belief, passion and hard work. He really believed in people and tried to put them into situations where they could do their jobs and then succeed. The guy was brilliant. He had a passion for the game unlike anything I have ever seen. I remember one time in New Jersey he called my hotel room at like 2:30 in the morning. I said, 'what the heck are you doing, I am sound asleep?' He said, 'take out a pencil and a piece of paper and write these lines down, then tell me what you think of them tomorrow in practice.' I mean he would think about hockey all the time, it consumed him. And he had so many innovative ideas. When he went to the NHL he was light years ahead of anybody else. People used to tell him that his ideas wouldn't work at that level, but he proved them wrong. He truly changed the game."

ON LEADERS & MANAGERS...

"The business world must produce more leaders not managers. Leadership is all about change, and all about the process of transforming organizations so that creativity and innovation are encouraged and can thrive. Good management is not enough by itself. There is a distinction. Managing is taking care of what has already been created. Leadership is, on the other hand, moving forward to create something new. Not all managers are leaders. Leaders tell us not what is, but what can be."
— *Herb Brooks*

CH. 14) LOYALTY WILL OPEN DOORS FOR YOU; WHETHER YOU CHOOSE TO WALK THROUGH THOSE DOORS IS UP TO YOU

Over the next several years, Brooks kept an open mind regarding his next career moves. He wanted to help grow the game at the amateur and youth levels, so he focused much of his attention on grass roots issues. He also got back into the game as a scout with the NHL's Pittsburgh Penguins. Later, when they needed him to take over as the team's head coach, he didn't let them down. Brooks would also use that opportunity to further his own cause as well, to clean up the game and make it better from the top down.

The next chapter of Herbie's life was all about growing the game from the grass-roots level and trying to make a difference. He would go back to the private sector for the next several years, addressing local youth hockey needs and trying to better the game. Brooks was a man with many causes and he enjoyed moving mountains in order to better those causes. He knew that it all started with the kids though and he wanted to do his part to make the game a better one. He was committed to getting more opportunities to more kids, at all levels of the game.

Brooks continued to do TV analysis and motivational speaking over the next couple of years, eventually reuniting with his old friend, Craig Patrick, in 1996. Patrick had just taken over as the general manager of the Pittsburgh Penguins and asked Herb if he was interested in becoming a full-time scout for the organization. Anxious to get back into the game, he agreed. Scouting was fun for Brooks, who was an excellent judge of both talent and character. He enjoyed working with young people and watching them develop. It would be a new adventure that was fun for him.

What wasn't fun, however, was all the traveling that came with it. As a scout, it wouldn't be uncommon for him to be gone for weeks at a time, trekking through such far away locales as Scandinavia, eastern Europe or the Soviet republics. Long road trips from Minnesota through the Canadian countrysides were usually the norm, however. He knew that if he was going to get another shot in the NHL, that he would have to keep his nose in the game. There were a lot of lonely nights in dump hotels from Moose Jaw to Moncton, but it was work that had to be done. He didn't mind though, he was happy to pay his dues.

Then, in what many dubbed as either a temporary moment of insanity or maybe even a midlife crisis, Brooks shocked the hockey world yet again by agreeing to become the head coach of the French

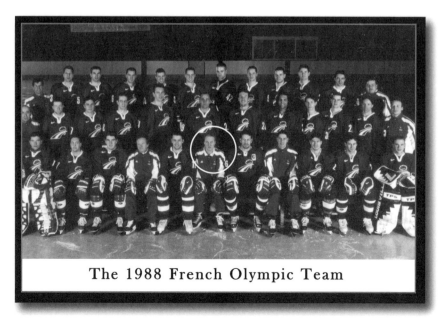

The 1988 French Olympic Team

Olympic team at the 1998 Winter Games in Nagano, Japan. Brooks was bored and needed a new challenge. And, maybe more importantly, he wanted to prove to USA Hockey that he could still coach.

Incredibly, that May his French squad came out and upset Team USA, 3-1, in the World Championships just prior to the Winter Games. Needless to say, Herbie definitely made his point to the powers-that-be at USA Hockey with that statement. As a result, the Americans would have to requalify for the Olympics, which they ultimately did a short while later. Team France, meanwhile, would finish with a 1-2 record in Nagano, eventually defeating Italy, 5-1, in the 11th-place game.

Brooks returned home and resumed his scouting career with the Penguins after that. He had become more involved with the team's player personnel decisions at this point and was enjoying the work. More importantly, he knew that he was making a difference and that his opinions mattered. A year went by and then, on an otherwise normal day in early December, Patti got a call from Penguin's GM, Craig Patrick. There was not much time for small talk, he needed to speak with Herbie right away. Patti told him that he had just stepped out to get the oil changed in his car. Patrick then asked if she knew the number to the place. She told him to hold on for a moment and then gave him the number to Automotive Services, in Maplewood, "home of the $19.95 express lube."

Sure enough, he called and asked the attendant to put Herbie on the phone. From there, Patrick proceeded to tell Herbie that he was making a coaching change and that he was going to be firing Kevin Constantine. He then said he wanted him to take the job and that he needed him in Pittsburgh as soon as humanly possible. In fact, there was a game that next night, and he wanted him to be behind the bench for it. Herb was speechless. He asked if he could have a little time to think about it, but Patrick said no. He told him that the Washington Capitals would be in town in less than 24 hours and that he needed him there.

And just like that, Herbie was back in the "show." He was very loyal and if his old friend Craig needed him, he was there for him. With that, Brooks went home and packed. Patti had been through the routine several times before. Heck, she probably figured that she would see more of him as an NHL head coach than she did while he had been circumnavigating the globe as a scout. He grabbed the next flight out of town to Pittsburgh and was thrilled to be embarking on his next great adventure.

Brooks wasted little time in making some noise in the Steel City, shutting-out the Caps that next night, 3-0. He had been out of the game as a coach for several years and figured he had a lot of catching up to do. So, he immersed himself into the new challenge and was determined to seize the moment. He had no illusions that there would be a fat long-term deal waiting for him at the end of the rainbow, so he just tried to work with what he had and have some fun.

The Penguins, led by All-Star forward Jaromir Jagr, were loaded with talent. And, like Jagr, many of the team's top players were from across the pond. In fact, 12 of the 21 skaters on the team were Europeans. Translation: they were familiar with the wide open, creative attacking style of hockey that Brooks was known for. The team won 10 of its next 14 games under Brooks and things were looking good with regards to making the post-season. They would go through their share of ups and downs over the ensuing months, but then came together in the end when it mattered.

One of the ways Brooks was able to earn the respect of his players was for them to know that he always had their backs, no matter what. Well, there was an incident that took place in mid-January that proved just that. During a game one night against the Avalanche in Denver, Pittsburgh's Matthew Barnaby was cross-checked with a cheap and dangerous hit late in the third period. There was no penalty call by the refs. Herb was upset, but he didn't want to make a big deal about it until he saw the tape after the game.

So, as they were watching the replay, Brooks heard Colorado's play-by-play announcer, John Kelly, say that he thought Barnaby had a tendency to "embellish" in those types of situations. Herb was now really pissed off, so he went outside the dressing room and confronted Kelly right on the spot. As Herb would later say, "I lost it." After a profani-

ON CHANGE...

"Change is one of those words as a coach you learn to hate. When a coach hears a general manager talk about a team needing change, it's time to get the bags packed. The same thing happens in politics. When the American people want change they elect a new President. Time will tell what kind of change we will get with a new coach in the White House. But changing a coach isn't always the answer. Sometimes, the way to turn a team around is to find a player who's a little better at killing penalties; or to recruit a center who can raise the level of play on an entire line; or to find the skater who cares a little more, works a little harder and demands a little more from himself and his teammates. I can't help but think that the same holds true for our government.

"Maybe coaches and Presidents have something in common, that they get too much credit in the good times and too much blame in the bad times. What our government really needs are politicians who are committed to getting things done. Men and women who seek office not to launch a career, but to share what they have learned from successful experiences in other walks of life. Maybe what we need in Congress are men and women who care a little more, work a little harder and demand a little more from themselves and their teammates."
                                                        — *Herb Brooks*

ty-laced tirade, which apparently involved a little extra-curricular shove, Brooks returned to the locker room, where his players genuinely appreciated what he had done. Was this another one of Herbie's psychological ploys? We'll never know for sure, but it certainly woke up his players and endeared him to them even more.

Unfortunately, the NHL brass didn't share those sentiments and suspended the coach for two games without pay for his actions. Brooks would later express his regret for the incident during a meeting with NHL Commissioner Gary Bettman, who had summoned the coach to meet with him afterwards. There, however, Brooks decided to use that valuable face time to give the commish an earful about some of the issues which he felt were ruining the game, specifically all of the needless obstruction that was smothering the league's most talented players — especially Jagr. He warned Bettman that if nothing was done soon, that they were running the risk of having all of the life being sucked right out of the game. He later sent him very detailed suggestions on how to improve the game, most of which were the impetus behind the NHL lock-out that ultimately canceled the 2004-05 season.

Meanwhile, Brooks continued to demand hard work, speed and excitement from his players. He insisted that they go out and have the times of their lives. Hockey was a fun game and he wanted them to start having fun again. They responded by rallying back from their lousy start and finished strong with a respectable 29-23-5 record (38-30-14 overall), good for third place in the very competitive Atlantic Division. Along the way, Brooks even won his 200th career NHL game. He just seemed to be a bit more relaxed this time around the coaching carousel, and it showed.

"I remember one time when Herbie was coaching in Pittsburgh, I came down to the locker room to talk to him before the game," recalled former Gopher Joe Micheletti, who went on to become a very successful TV analyst. "Now, it was a pretty big playoff game, and I was trying to get ready to go on the air and I figured Herb would be nervous and getting ready to go too. Well, I go down there and instead of talking hockey, he starts talking about the stock market. He knew that I used to be in that business, so he liked to talk about new stocks and what not with me. So, he brings over the chalk board and proceeds to break down three different high tech companies, one by one, telling me the pros and cons of each company and what their long term forecast was in his opinion. He goes into this 20 minute dissertation about these companies and I was just blown away. Then, when he was all done, he erased the board and started talking hockey, diagramming plays like nothing had just happened. I mean the guy was just brilliant, and was intensely passionate about everything he did in life, no matter what it was. That was just classic Herbie. He even won the game that night too."

From there, the Penguins advanced on to the playoffs, where they beat the Washington Capitals, four games to one, in the Eastern Conference Quarterfinals. They then met up with their inter-state rivals, the Philadelphia Flyers, in the conference semis in what would turn out

This was a letter that Herbie sent to NHL Commissioner
Gary Bettman about his ideas regarding rule changes.
Prophetically, most of the changes came to fruition
following the league-wide lock-out of 2004-05:

MR. GARY BETTMAN
COMMISSIONER
NATIONAL HOCKEY LEAGUE
1251 AVENUE OF THE AMERICAS
47TH FLOOR
NEW YORK, NY 10020-1198

DEAR MR. BETTMAN:

IN FEBRUARY 1993 WHEN YOU BECAME THE COMMISSIONER OF THE NHL, I WAS COACHING
THE NEW JERSEY DEVILS. AT THAT TIME I WROTE YOU A LETTER WITH SUGGESTIONS TO
IMPROVE THE NHL GAME. AFTER READING STATEMENTS BY MARIO LEMIEUX AT HIS HALL
OF FAME INDUCTION, AND MOST RECENTLY BY BRETT HULL, I WOULD LIKE TO REVISIT MY
THOUGHTS.

AS YOU KNOW THE NHL IS IN THE ENTERTAINMENT BUSINESS. PURE AND SIMPLE. THE
ATHLETES ARE THE PERFORMERS. THEY DRIVE THE VALUE AND PRODUCE THE "ROI" FOR
THE CONSUMER AND THE INVESTORS.

THE GAME IS PLAYED ON ICE. NOT GRASS-BLACKTOP-OR WOOD. WITHOUT A DOUBT,
HOCKEY IS THE FASTEST MOST EXCITING GAME PLAYED. TO REDUCE THE GAME TO A SLOW
PLODDING BORING GAME DOES NOBODY-FANS, PLAYERS, OWNERS-ANY GOOD.

I WOULD LIKE TO SUGGEST AGAIN, IN THE SPIRIT OF PROGRESS, ONE VITAL RULE CHANGE.
MOVE THE GOAL LINE OUT TO 15 FEET FROM THE END BOARDS. REDUCE THE WIDTH OF
THE NEUTRAL ZONE ACCORDINGLY, AS MOST OF THE GAME IS PLAYED IN THE END ZONES
ANYWAY. THIS WILL ELIMINATE ALOT OF THE "SCRUMS" AND SLOW PLAY IN THE CORNERS.
FOCUS ON THE PLAYERS TALENTS INSTEAD OF PUTTING FANS TO SLEEP.

REGARDING THE RED LINE, THAT IS AN OPTION. USE IT FOR ICING ONLY AND ELIMINATE
THE TWO LINE PASS, OR KEEP IT THE SAME. MOVING THE GOAL LINE OUT SHOULD NOT BE
AN OPTION.

MR. BETTMAN, WHEN CRAIG PATRICK AND I JOINED THE NEW YORK RANGERS SOME YEARS
AGO, WE PUT IN AN ENTIRELY DIFFERENT STYLE OF PLAY WITH THE PUCK. ONE THAT
WOULD BRING OUT THE TRUE AND INNATE TALENTS OF THE PLAYERS. ONLY THE
EDMONTON OILERS, UNDER GLEN SATHER, PLAYED THE SAME WAY. AT THAT TIME I SAID,
"MOVE THE GOAL LINE OUT TO 15 FEET AND ELIMINATE THE RED LINE."

TODAY, THE PLAYERS ARE BIGGER THAN EVER. MORE ICE SPACE IS NEEDED TO KEEP FAN
INTEREST. RESCIND THE "EDMONTON" RULE AND GO BACK TO FOUR ON FOUR PLAY.
NOBODY LIKES CHANGE, BUT THERE IS NO PROGRESS WITHOUT IT.

LOOK AT WHAT YOU AND YOUR COLLEAGUES DID AT THE NBA. THE THREE POINT SHOT. THE
TWENTY FOUR SECOND SHOT CLOCK. LOOK AT THE RESULTS. HELP GIVE THE GAME BACK
TO THE PLAYERS. MAYBE MARIO WOULD NOT HAVE LEFT.

RESPECTFULLY,

HERB BROOKS

VINDICATION...

Herbie always felt very strongly about growing the game the *right* way. Change was a good thing in his eyes, because he knew that the game was always evolving from era to era. He was particularly critical of the National Hockey League, which he felt needed to take drastic actions to keep up with the times.

"I have written to Mr. Bettman on several occasions to express my opinions on several matters of change within the NHL such as eliminating the red line and moving the goal line out," said Brooks. "The players are bigger, faster and stronger and the game is not keeping up. Hey, we are in the entertainment business. Is it right to ask fans to pay $100 bucks to be put to sleep?"

Herb's son, Dan, had his own take on that situation as well as his father's desire to constantly improve the game, even if that meant ruffling some feathers: "It's amazing when you think about it, but my dad was right on with his predictions in that letter," he said. "Almost all of the things he talked about in it came to fruition following the NHL lock-out. My dad bucked heads a lot with the hockey powers-that-be over the years. He needed to have an enemy, or adversarial force in his life at all times; that was very important to him I think. When he was coaching, obviously that manifested itself as the competition on any one given evening. But, when he had causes or issues that he felt needed to be addressed in order to better the game, then those people or groups became the enemy. In this case, it was the NHL, because the rules were old and outdated and the game was changing and evolving around them."

"My dad loved hockey and did whatever he could to make the game better. If there were problems that he saw at the youth levels or at the high school levels, then he would take on USA Hockey, the governing body which oversees those things. He just always wanted to grow and better the game, and was willing to do whatever he thought was necessary to do so. He wanted the game to be more grass roots in nature and run more at the local levels. He rubbed a lot of people the wrong way during his crusades too, a lot of people. But, because of his notoriety and political clout, he was able to get things done. He loved it when people challenged him on issues, because that would only add fuel to his fire. He definitely burned a lot of bridges along the way though, no question. As far as the lock-out went, I only wish my dad had been alive to see that his ideas were heard because the changes that were made are great for the game."

to be a classic. There, the Pens went up two games to none, and then saw the series get tied at two games apiece when Philadelphia's Keith Primeau's notched the game-winning goal at the 92:01 mark of the fifth overtime session to end what would become the third-longest game in Stanley Cup playoff history. With the momentum now swung the other way, the Flyers then went on to win the thrilling series in seven games. It was a bitter ending to an otherwise unbelievable season.

Herbie had fun that season though and certainly proved he was every bit of the turnaround specialist that he had become known as. For Brooks, however, that was it. He had no contract, no promises and no deal, just a handshake with Patrick and team owner, Mario Lemieux. Patrick would later offer Brooks a contract to become the team's full-time head coach. It was a good offer, not a great one, but one Brooks was willing to say no to nonetheless.

Here is how Herb's son, Dan, recalled the situation: "I remember when Craig offered him the head coaching job with the Penguins" said Dan. "My dad said he would take it if he could get paid what he thought was fair. He said he wanted the average salary of a typical third line forward, about a million bucks a year at that time. They came close, but in the end didn't give it to him. The franchise was in bankruptcy at the time and it was not a great time to be playing hard ball, but my dad stuck to his guns. There were a lot of other coaches with worse records making a lot more. So, he said screw it, just out of principle.

"Who knows? Had he taken that and then had success, he could have been making several million dollars a year within a few seasons. He was sort of a martyr though and was only willing to do things on his own terms. For better or worse, you have to admire and respect that. It is amazing to think how much money my dad could have made had he stuck with it though. I mean that man left a lot of money on the table. But, he didn't want to coach for the sake of money. He was always looking for the right opportunity and wasn't willing to compromise his principles for that. I respect that a lot, but I also have to wonder how different life would be if he would have been a little more flexible in that regard."

CH. 15) DARE TO DREAM BIG;
AND WHEN YOU DO, GO FOR THE GOLD

Brooks took a leap of faith in 2002 when he agreed to take over as the head coach of the U.S. Olympic team which would be competing at the Winter Games in Salt Lake City, Utah. It was a big risk, but Brooks knew that USA Hockey needed a boost in order to keep growing the base of the pyramid, especially for young boys and girls at the youth levels. So, he embraced the situation and once again, made America proud.

After respectfully declining the offer to coach the Penguins that next season, Brooks went back to scouting. It was much less stressful and it allowed him more time to spend with his family back home. Spending time with the grandkids was what the next chapter of Brooks' storied career was going to be all about, and he wanted to keep his options open.

Then, early in 2001, a bizarre 4 a.m., phone call changed all of that. Herbie had been sound asleep in his South Bend, Ind., hotel room, where he was in town for a scouting trip. Startled, the groggy Brooks picked up the receiver.

"Hello?"
"Herb, you've got to coach the 2002 Olympic team in Salt Lake City..."

That was it, no "hello," no "this is so-and-so," nothing. Herb knew who it was and he promptly blurted back: "Sheehy, you're either crazy or you're drunk...". Turned out he was neither.

Yes, it was former NHL player-turned agent and close friend Neil Sheehy, who sat sleepless in a Florida hotel room tossing and turning that night thinking about hockey. There was something on his mind and it couldn't wait until morning. He knew that he was going to have to use some "Herbie psychology" on the master psychologist himself, so he jumped right in.

"I could tell he was intrigued by the idea," recalled Sheehy. "Well, we had a bunch of blow-ups over it over the next few weeks, but eventually he agreed. I can remember on several occasions him just melting down with USA Hockey, and him calling me to say 'Neil, if they don't want me, then that's it! I am out. I am done, that's it!' So, then I started writing him notes on why he should take the job."

"One of them read: 'Herb, if you are serious about coaching, seize this moment. If you prefer to sell long distance service or sporting goods, respectfully decline and continue selling. *(Brooks had offers he was mulling over at the time regarding other business ventures.)* If you are more interested in selling Christian Brothers Hockey Sticks than in being behind the bench, then forget about this short term coaching opportunity, because it is not worth it. If you want to watch a few games a year and spend three months a year in Florida golfing, forget that I thought this was a good opportunity, it's not worth it.

"If you don't get a thrill by directing 20 men into war and teaching them to believe in themselves for the benefit of each other by winning, forget that I called you at four in the morning, thinking that this was a good idea, it wasn't. I believe that if you really want something in life, you do everything in your power and give everything in your belly to get it. It may not happen, but the effort was worth it. If you don't care to coach again, forget about it, it is not worth it. You have a tremendous God-given ability to influence people to believe, the only tragedy I see is that I am not sure that you believe. I do not believe that there is a better coach on this planet than you, I want to make the journey with you. Seize

136

the moment. But, if you do not believe, forget it. It is not worth it.'

"He called me right after that and told me that I was a no good son-of-a-bitch and that he was ticked off. He thought he was the only one who knew how to play mind games. But hey, the next thing you know he got back into coaching. It was a great story."

Brooks was always up for a good challenge, and Sheehy's psyche-job was just the shove Herbie needed to get back into the game. Sheehy had been able to push just the right buttons to get him all fired up, borrowing a page right out of Herbie's infamous reverse psychology book. With that, Herbie patched up his on-again-off-again relationship with USA Hockey, and on Nov. 1, 2001, he was named as the head coach of the U.S. Olympic team which would compete at the 2002 Winter Games in Salt Lake City, Utah.

USA Hockey knew that Brooks was stubborn, headstrong and opinionated, but they also knew that they needed him desperately. The program had been on life support in recent years and they were hoping he would be able to resuscitate it back to its glory days. Plus, with Team USA's embarrassing performance both on and off the ice at the Winter Games in Nagano, Japan, back in 1998, they desperately needed some good P.R. They weren't saying it publicly, but they were praying for another Miracle. This time around, however, things would be much different. Gone were the college kids and in were the NHL All-Stars. The rules of the game had changed, but as usual, Herbie would be up for the challenge.

"I'm extremely interested in the American hockey movement, and if USA Hockey feels I can help in this capacity at this time, I'm very proud to do so," Brooks would say. "The Olympics are special and transcend other sporting events. Although the competition will be extremely difficult, I believe in the American players in the National Hockey League and their competitive spirit. They'll play hard and smart, and they'll make a very good showing, one that we can all be proud of."

As far as the NHL All-Star "dream team" was concerned, that was a concept Brooks was not particularly thrilled about to say the least.

ON DREAMS AND DREAMERS...

"We are the makers of dreams, the dreamers of dreams. We should be dreaming. We grew up as kids having dreams, but now we're too sophisticated as adults, as a nation. We stopped dreaming. We should always have dreams. I'm a dreamer."
— *Willie Wonka*

— *A line from Herbie's favorite movie* —
"Willie Wonka and the Chocolate Factory"

"To me the Olympics are not about 'dream teams,' they're more about dreamers," said Brooks. "They're not about medals, but the pursuit of medals. The Olympics are not about being No. 1, they're about sacrificing and trying to be No. 1."

"As far as the argument over whether it should be amateurs or pros playing, I will say that while I do understand the business side with regards to visibility, marketing and dollars, I also have to say that it is unfortunate that if a kid wants to one day play on an Olympic team, he has to first become an NHL All-Star," he added. "But that is all part of change and while it is debatable, this is where we are at and we will make the best of it."

What Brooks did enjoy, however, was a new adventure. And this was going to be just that, which excited him tremendously. He knew that even temperamental and arrogant millionaires all had one common denominator: they played the game because of the little boy inside them. Brooks' job was simply going to be to find that little boy. He also had an ulterior motive.

"I'm doing it for the cause," Brooks told the Minneapolis Star Tribune, shortly before the Games began. "And the cause is this: Hopefully our Olympic team will be an impetus and a catalyst to further the growth of American hockey. I've seen American players go from the apprentice in the game, to the journeyman in the game, to some real masters of the trade. I want to continue to see that growth, and this is a vehicle to do that."

From there, Brooks had the awesome responsibility of selecting his team. And, just like he had done back in 1980, he started researching and assembling lists. He would dive into the task at hand and leave no stone unturned. He called dozens and dozens of his former players to get their opinions and feedback. Preparation was Herb's forte and he took the situation very seriously. His assistant coach, Lou Vairo, who had served as the head coach of the 1984 U.S. Olympic team, remembered the selection process this way:

"Herb was a good detail man," said Vairo. "He was a fierce competitor. He was also a very good judge of talent and character. And, obviously he had good players, because no coach wins without talented players. But, he knew how to put it all together and could motivate his players like no one I had ever seen. He was just a tremendous leader too. He took charge and got things done. There was no secret. He just worked hard and was real intelligent. In fact, that might have been the thing that was the most impressive about him, his intelligence."

"Then, I was also really impressed by the thoroughness that he exhibited with regards to scouting players. I mean he hated to cut people, so he would fly back and forth across the country, three or four times, to see guys play as much as he could. He just didn't want to make a mistake and pick anybody for his team that wasn't deserving. Then, we would have discussions about players for hours on end, debating every little detail about them and what they could bring to the table. He was very good too about listening to everybody's input and valuing their opinions. You know, there were some really good players that he wasn't able to select for that 2002 team and that tore him up inside. He knew that those players would take it personally, and that hurt him. But, he was the boss and he knew that he had to make some tough decisions. Herb was a gamer, and I totally respected that about him."

The XIX Olympic Winter Games then got underway with an Opening Ceremonies tribute to the 1980 "Miracle on Ice." The entire team was secretly flown in to collectively light the Olympic caldron that night in a dramatic reenactment of their impromptu medal presentation celebration 22 years earlier. It was the first time the entire team had been together since that incredible day back in Lake Placid.

The one person who was conspicuously missing, however, was Herbie. Ironically, he had another, "more important," engagement that evening. You see, he had already committed to being at a retirement supper for one of his old pals at a VFW in North St. Paul. So, rather than having a rare moment in the limelight in front of a few billion people around the globe, he spent a quiet evening back in St. Paul with some of the fellas from the neighborhood. That was Herbie, the proud east sider who just never forgot where he came from. Plus, he didn't want to be up on that pedestal with the players, it was "their" time, and he wasn't about to impose. That was just not his style.

When the players finally hit the ice, there was a lot of buzz about Brooks being able to create another "Miracle." Herbie didn't care about

that stuff though, because he knew it was an entirely different situation this time around with the professional players. In fact, he only had a few days to prepare them for battle, unlike the 1980 team, which spent nearly eight months together. The NHL had agreed to allow the players to compete in the Games for a special two week hiatus during their regular season, so there was little time to get acquainted.

"The parallels between 1980 and 2002 were not even close," said Brooks. "In 1980 it was a bunch of college kids. We were trying to take them out of their comfort zone of being college athletes, college All-Americans, and play at a certain tempo of world class competition in the Olympic Games. But this (the NHLers) is a different thing. I'm not going to be introducing a lot of things to these athletes. I'm not going to be telling them things they don't already know. They all come from good programs and have had excellent coaches. It's more of a reminder. It's really their show. The strategy comes down to how well we adapt to the different styles. The Europeans, who play on larger ice sheets, have more finesse players, while the North Americans play a much more physical game."

Still, Brooks' legacy was alive and well with the group. Most of the American players were products of the "Miracle on Ice," in that they were just kids when it happened and had gotten hooked on the game even more so upon its thrilling outcome. The players knew Herbie and they respected him. They knew that he was a master at strategizing on

the wide ice open ice surface that was unique to the international game. They were grateful for the hard work he had done for USA Hockey and were going to give it their all to try and win another gold medal. It didn't take long for them to transform to a Brooks-like squad either. Their practice sessions were crisp; the players were working extremely hard on the fundamentals; and they were genuinely excited to be there representing their country.

Team USA opened the Games by blanking Finland, 6-0, in the opener; tied Russia, 2-2, in Game Two; pounded Belarus, 8-1, in Game Three; shut out Germany, 5-1, in Game Four; and then beat Russia, 3-2, in the semifinals to advance to the gold medal round against Canada. The Russian game was thrilling and brought back a lot of memories from the icy Miracle. They jumped out to a 3-0 lead in that one and then hung on for dear life down the stretch. Defenseman Phil Housley notched what proved to be the game-winner and goalie Mike Richter played outstanding in the nets, holding off one final Russian barrage at the buzzer.

From there, the team would face the best in the business, Team Canada. When asked about what he thought of the Canadians just prior to the game, Brooks played it safe. You see, Brooks was working as a scout for Pittsburgh at the time, and Team Canada's captain just happened to be Penguins owner, Mario Lemieux. Said Brooks jokingly, "Well, Mario is my boss, so I'd just like to say I think Canada is a really great team."

Hockey fans everywhere were thrilled to see the Americans and Canadians go to battle in the Finals. It had been more than 50 years since a gold medal had presided north of the border, and they were not going to just roll over. Brooks was up for the challenge though, and when Tony Amonte put the U.S. up 1-0 at 8:49 of the first period, the crowd went wild. The TV ratings for the game were tremendous too, as it all played out on prime time across North America.

Canada roared back to make it 2-1 after the first period, only to see Team USA winger Brian Rafalski beat goalie Martin Brodeur at the 15:30 mark to tie it up on a power-play goal. Canada's Joe Sakik put the Red Shirts ahead for good just a few minutes later, as Team Canada poured it on from there and went on to win the game, 5-2. The game was much closer than the final score would indicate though, as Brett Hull and Mike Modano had some quality scoring chances in the final minutes of the game. But in the end it was too little too late as the Americans just couldn't catch a break. It was destiny for the Canadians, who rejoiced at center ice as the final buzzer sounded. Brooks would have to settle for a silver this time, a bittersweet consolation for what turned out to be some truly amazing hockey.

Fans from across the country got behind the team as Brooks made Americans fall in love with hockey all over again. Perhaps another generation of little kids were watching and will be the stars of Team USA in another decade or two? That was certainly the hope for Brooks. It had been a full circle journey for the legendary coach, who had once again made America proud. Believe it or not, some had even questioned his motives, to which he had this reply:

"You know, someone asked me at a seminar why I would coach the 2002 Olympic Hockey team after winning the gold medal in 1980, and risk losing credibility," Brooks would recall shortly after the Games. "I told him that I was a psychology major in college and asked if he was familiar with Sigmund Freud. Some of Freud's writings dealt with people who avoid stress, competition and anxiety, oftentimes tranquilizing themselves. They wind up sort of sleep-walking through life, never really understanding their true capabilities. So, I guess I never wanted to step away from a challenge, and I am very glad I did it. We came up just short in that gold medal game against Canada, but it was a marvelous experience. I am much better off for having taken on that challenge. That is what life is all about."

When it was all said and done, not only was the nation grateful for his service, but so too were the players. One of those players was playing in the Minnesota State High School Hockey Tournament back in the Winter of 1980 and was thrilled to be able to play for one of the game's most legendary coaches.

"I was so lucky to get to play for him so late in my career," said 21-year NHL veteran defenseman Phil Housley. "I had always hoped to play for him, and to finally get that opportunity in 2002 meant a great deal to me. He chose me to be on that team, and to be the only Minnesota player meant the world to me. He had to make some tough

decisions and I was fortunate to be selected by him. It was a real honor. You know, when I scored the game-winner over Russia in the semifinals, it made me feel even better about the fact that Herbie had picked me and that I was able to be on his team. That was an unbelievable experience."

ON SUCCESS...

"Success is not a destination, but a route you must travel. The ingredients for success include the intangibles, the spirit of a team, the strength of association and the power we generate as we work as a unit. These, I firmly believe, are the ingredients that propel any successful organization or team."   — *Herb Brooks*

FIVE STEPS TO SUCCESS:
1. Determine your strengths and weaknesses.
2. Pick your opportunities.
3. Set goals, long and short range, and then write them down.
4. Work hard.
5. Have fun. After all, if the first four steps have been done correctly, then there's nothing you'd rather be doing.

ON SELF-MOTIVATION...

"If you're having motivational problems, it's a sure bet you're having performance problems as well. Motivation is the energy that makes everything work. It is clearly the single most critical factor in performance.

"Why do athletes or workers lose their motivation? What causes players or workers to burn out and lose interest? At the most basic level, this occurs because performing no longer fulfills or promises to fulfill their basic psychological needs. The needs for recognition, approval, self-worth or success. In fact, quite the opposite may be occurring. So what can be done to maintain high levels of self motivation, and, what can we do to get it back when it's lost? The answer comes as no surprise...success.

"It is not success through the eyes of someone else. It is success as perceived from the point of view of the worker himself that becomes the deciding force. The facts are clear, so long as you see yourself succeeding, moving ever closer toward the realization of another meaningful goal for yourself, then you will stay motivated. The right connection pairs success, not with winning the external contest, but with effort, accomplishment and forward growth. The key to motivation is steady success.

"Why then does anyone stay with it? What's the payoff that makes it all worthwhile and keeps you motivated? The answer, in a word, is the challenge. It's having a dream of what you might do or become with yourself, and inching forward each day toward the realization of that dream.

"Have a dream, a dream of what you could possibly achieve. Every good athlete I've known first had a dream of being No. 1. What is your dream? Everything first begins and eventually takes shape from a dream, then into a purpose, then goal setting, then preparation and finally persistency.

"There's also another side to the business of setting goals that hasn't been discussed yet. That simply is that whenever you set goals for yourself, you can also create problems, conflicts and hard work. You're putting yourself on the line. You are risking failure and you are creating mountains of hard work.

"You're also creating lots of problems for yourself, problems of anxiety and tension, of controlling your anger and temper, of staying positive and optimistic, of managing mistakes, of handling failure, of time, of money, and many other things. You put yourself on the line. You took a chance. But that's what it takes to be a winner. Taking risks, making mistakes and then finally breaking through."
                                                            – Herb Brooks

CH. 16) WHAT'S YOUR PASSION? DEFINE IT; OWN IT; AND THEN STAND BEHIND IT.

Herb Brooks had a passion for the sport of hockey. He loved everything about it. In fact, he loved it so much that he was willing to do whatever it took in order to make sure that the game grew and expanded what he felt was the right way, with respect. Sometimes his wasn't the most popular voice, but he made sure it was heard nonetheless, because he wanted his passion to be enjoyed by future generations the way he had enjoyed it as a young boy on St. Paul's east side.

When the dust finally settled following the hoopla surrounding the Olympics, Herbie was able to sit down and reflect upon what he really wanted in life. Personally, he was happy. Professionally, he knew that there was still much work to be done with regards to growing the game he so dearly loved. When asked about the state-of-the-state of hockey in America at that time, this is how he responded:

"Overall, there has been great progress in American hockey over the past 25 years or so," said Brooks. "For us to keep on moving forward though, we really need to encourage the debate, the dialogue and the discussion for change. We should be respectful of one another, understand differing philosophies, and work together to make American hockey better. We have so many great athletes in our country and I think that our future is unbelievable. We just have to work on our developmental programs and keep it going. I do think there are too many AAA, showcase and elite camps, etc., for young kids today and as a result we are creating a bunch of robots. We need to make it fun for our kids and let them learn to love this game the way we did. Kids love to play and we need to give this game back to them. Our coaches need to make practices more fun by making drills that are both fun and competitive, that will challenge the kids to find the games within the game. We are doing a great job though. Our girls programs are continually getting better, we're getting more and more kids onto the next levels and the rest will eventually take care of itself."

"We have the infrastructure in place, we have a lot of wonderful volunteers and we have some very dedicated coaches out there. But I think we have to always remember, at least on the amateur side, what this is for. It is for our young people so that they have a real meaningful environment to play and learn the game. There are a lot of positive things, but we also have to watch out for the 'doing too much too soon for too few' syndrome. Basically, we need to stop narrowing the base of our pyramid. We have to understand that when you have competition without preparation, then there is no real development. Sure, we've got to take care of our elite players by challenging them and bringing them along, but at the same time we can't let other kids, with latent development, fall through the cracks. And these triple A programs, showcase teams, and select programs do little for the real developmental of our players. That is a big concern.

"Another problem is that a lot of our kids have nowhere to go after high school. I mean we are turning out kids, bringing them up and increasing participation, but then all of a sudden they get to a certain level and there are no more opportunities for them. As a result, too many good kids are being forced out of the game way too early. That is where college club hockey comes in. Right now there are roughly 200 schools playing club hockey. Now, I think that it would be incredible if we could start to get some more of these programs to make that jump to D-I varsity status. That is really what the game needs right now. It would not only get more kids playing hockey, it would build the game's fan base, and the game would expand to more of a nationwide game. Who knows? Maybe one day Georgia Tech will be playing Southern Cal for the national championship? Wouldn't that be something? So, overall we need to reach down and help to create more opportunities for our players. And by helping them, we are helping ourselves by growing the game and ultimately growing the pyramid's base even wider. This is another key area where the NHL could step in and help financially to grow the game at this level.

"We also have to ask ourselves why the Europeans are producing so much talent these days? Well, in Europe they have a better ratio of games to practices, and in the United States we are turning out a bunch of 20-minute hockey players. That is a serious problem. Think about it. It takes an hour for kids to get to the rink and get ready. They play one-third of the one hour game for a total of 20 minutes, and then it takes another hour to get undressed and go home. That means a kid is only playing 20-minutes of hockey out of a three-hour afternoon.

"The bottom line is that we need more emphasis on development, pure and simple, and one way to achieve that is by hiring professional coaches who can coach other coaches. Sure, we have coaching clinics and certification programs, but is it enough? Now, this is in no way intended to be a back-handed slap at our youth coaches and volunteers who are giving up their time and energy to help teach our kids. Rather, it is something to consider to help our kids get better. If a program were to hire a young professional coach to help teach and train the

KEY-NOTE SPEECH FOR IBM

"I'm always a little nervous when I speak to IBM. IBM is a world leader, a company with such prestige, so many top level people and such high standards. Your chairman told me to relax, working for IBM is 80% mental, and if you conquer it mentally, you've got 50% of it beat!

"I'm not here to be funny, or maybe I should say, attempting to be funny. I have been assigned a topic, to relate sales to athletics. I've been in sales and I've been in athletics, and there's a definite relationship. You sell a product, I sell X's and O's. But a product or the tactics of a team are not sold unless there is belief, a belief in the product and a belief in the system. The bottom line is personal motivation.

"Motivation, positive thinking and communication: how many books have been written? How many cassettes have been made? How many seminars have been given? Why is motivation such a big topic today? I believe it is because we have such a high standard of living. An individual does not have to extend himself too far to lead a relatively good life nowadays.

"Did you know I was not the first person chosen to coach the 1980 U.S. Olympic team? The first man declined because of the fact that there were too many problems to overcome. When I was interviewed, the USOC asked me why I would want to accept this job that meant coaching a team which would be the youngest in the U.S. history, and that was seeded only seventh?

"I quoted George Bernard Shaw: 'You see things and say why? But, I dream things that never were and say, why not? For if you study history ladies and gentlemen, you will find that the Greeks 500 years before Christ taught us the best things are the most difficult.' That was the fuel for my motivation.

"I have seen too many people, business or otherwise, that run from problems or a competitive environment. To me, I see it differently. A powerful success force can be created by the way you view a problem. I feel problems, struggles and obstacles have a hidden ingredient that makes them very effective in creating a success force. The word is 'opportunity.'

"I looked at Lake Placid as an opportunity. You have an opportunity as managers to excel. If you programmed yourself to view every problem as an opportunity, imagine what a powerful force you would apply to your life.

"Problems? I had problems, many problems. First, I had to convince the USOC that I had a plan. Then I had to convince them that we had to break tradition. I told them that we had to be aggressive, innovative and creative. I reminded them that this was 1980, not 1972 or 1968. Secondly, I had to convince the NHL GM's not to turn these young players pro and to let them compete for their country. Lastly, I had to convince the players themselves that we had a chance to excel.

"Lets face it. It's tough to be a coach and it's tough to be a manager. You're very visible. You're going to be critiqued in terms of the production of the entire group. You may be fired. You're going to be talked about, talked to, pushed and pulled. Let me tell you something about yourself. At all times it is necessary to put yourself in the shoes of your subjects. How would I like it if I was in his or her place?

"Ask that question over and over. Yes, recognize your problems and talk about your problems. But recognition and talking are still not enough.

"Our story was about hard work, togetherness and creativity. Is that not the same story of IBM? In our case we had to work hard to get on top. In your case, well, it is harder staying on top than getting there. I think we would all agree that people want to be successful, that's human nature. But wanting is not enough, there has to be more.

"Our success was based first upon our dreams. I encouraged our athletes to dream great dreams, but not to stop there. They had to have a will that translated those dreams into a reality. You have to have a will to win. I told them this in our first meeting we had out in Colorado Springs, a full eight months before Lake Placid.

"They had to let something inspire them; some goal, some cause, some great challenge. I told them to let something inspire them and to see themselves not for what they were, but for what they could become. I told them to play the game with the greatest abilities that were within them. Then, and only then, would they have peace of mind.

"Success is won by those who believe in winning and then prepare for that moment. Many want to win, but how many prepare? That is the big difference. A sound value system held water then, holds water today, and will hold water in the future.

"But still all the dreaming and preparation is not enough. After all our plans, our dreams, our preparation, it seemed as if it all went for naught the day before the Olympics when we got beat badly by the Russians in Madison Square Garden, 10-3. Our team was beaten not only physically, but also mentally. I said to our hockey team that a good butt kicking never hurt a quality athlete, and I believe it never hurts a quality organization either. If you're good and you have a quality product, you can come back. Our greatest glory was not in never falling, but in rising every time we fell. We came from behind to either win or tie in six of the seven games we played in the Olympics.

"Courage must be added to your dreams and preparations. We came from behind three times in the Russian game to win 4-3. That's courage. But it also takes courage to be a salesman. It means the willingness to suffer, to sacrifice, to work harder than the next fellow. It means you get home a little later, a little wearier, a little hungrier, and with a few more aches and pains. Maybe you considered quitting to go to an easier job, but you haven't. That's courage.

"My philosophy, ladies and gentlemen, is very basic: 'nobody can tell me I've accomplished enough.' You're in a highly competitive environment. Be very slow to believe that you are better than you are. 'It is a fatal but common mistake, for everyone that has been saved by a true estimation of another's weakness, many have been destroyed by a false appreciation of their own strength.'

"Too often today success is attributed solely to talent. Talent is the obvious ingredient of greatness, but the hidden ingredients are determination and dedication. As legendary Green Bay Packers Coach Vince Lombardi used to say, 'Talent is a gift, but it is more than that. It is a trust which no man has a right to ignore or worse still, abuse. Each man, whatever the degree of talent bestowed upon him, has a moral responsibility not only to himself, but to society, to develop that gift to its utmost.' I would agree."

— *Herb Brooks*

volunteer coaches at a grass-roots level, wouldn't that make everyone better? Now, does it cost money? Sure, but that is one area where the Europeans are advancing much quicker than we are and as a result they are producing more talent on to the next levels. I think we should open a dialogue and discuss it, that's all.

"We need to look at what Europe is doing to get better and try to get better ourselves. We need to make some changes and that can only be good for the game. Tolstoy once said 'Everybody wants to change the world, but they don't want to change themselves.' So, we all have to change our thinking and focus on getting our kids better. I have always been a student of the Europeans' philosophies and styles of hockey. Having said that I don't think that they are necessarily better athletes. They are just trained differently, with much more emphasis put on skill development, pace of execution and repetition. Are Europeans better athletes? No. Are they more competitive people? Certainly not. And, are their more opportunities for them? Not even close. I mean we have more rinks in Minnesota alone than in most of Europe. They work with what they've got though, and are not afraid to do exhaustive dry-land training to hone their skills.

"I remember watching a bunch of kids practicing on a basketball court in Czechoslovakia one time, working on their back cross-overs, their break-outs and on their power-play in just tennis shoes. They were mastering the spatial relationships and working with what they had. There are only a few rinks in all of Prague, so how do they produce so much top-level talent? It is strictly a matter of development and the way that they are introduced to the development sequence of skills that they learn.

"Lastly, we need to increase the number of rinks in America. Let's be real, arenas cost a lot of money, and I think there might be some more efficient uses of our hard-earned money to build them. Whenever a new arena is built there are hundreds of thousands of dollars that are appropriated to things that do not affect change or help the athletes or coaches. We need ice sheets, locker rooms and ice resurfacers. We don't always need, however, weight rooms, restaurants, beautiful lobbies and architectural niceties. Sure, they are nice, but they cost a lot of money. We have to ask ourselves, who are we building these for: the fans or for the kids? Perhaps instead of building such elaborate indoor facilities, we should go back to constructing more outdoor rinks with artificial ice. This is what baseball, soccer and basketball have over hockey — kids can hone their games virtually anywhere.

"Hockey is unique, we need ice. Sure, there are thousands of lakes and ponds, but the weather doesn't always cooperate. So we need more good quality outdoor ice sheets in order for our kids to get in more practice time. With girls hockey growing in popularity, ice-time has never been more scarce. This is another way to help out. So maybe the next time they want to build a community rink for $5 million, they should look instead to build 5 to 10 outdoor lighted artificial rinks, with warming houses, where kids could play consistently for six months out of the year. And, while youth associations could have structured practices here, it would also be a great place for kids to learn the game. Oftentimes that is where kids learn their creativity, playing pick-up games against other kids in an unstructured, informal environment with no coaches screaming at them."

Herb Brooks had a vision for how he wanted the game to grow and expand for future generations. He was willing to take unpopular stances in order to achieve those objectives too, which is what made him so unique. He clearly had a vision and led by example towards achieving that vision.

And, just like the scenario Brooks spoke of regarding the Europeans being able to do so much with so little, so too was his own childhood back in St. Paul. You see, Herbie grew up as a rink rat, playing the game on the outdoor ponds and rinks near Lake Phalen. Those east side kids eventually all funnelled into Johnson High School, which was the powerhouse team of the Twin Cities back in the 1950s and '60s. In fact, prior to 1965, Johnson was the only school south of Duluth to win a state hockey tournament, and they won a total of four.

And, just like with the European players scenario, did the Phalen rink rats have better facilities? No. Did they have better athletes? No. Did they have better coaches? Certainly not. In fact, Johnson's legendary coach didn't even know how to skate. The difference in Brooks' eyes was the fact that the community had created a culture which embraced the sport and made it fun for the kids. They provided plenty of "structured-unstructured" ice time for them in the form of outdoor rinks, and they supported them through grass roots programs that each local neighborhood could get behind.

Hockey became a social gathering for all of the hard working, blue collar workers, and acted as the glue which held it all together. The kids enjoyed playing the game and learned to play it the right way, with the bigger kids teaching the smaller ones. The game belonged to the kids and they embraced it. Everybody volunteered and supported the kids, because that was what it was all about. Because it was important to the parents, then that attitude trickled down to everybody else, especially to the kids — who learned to play the game with respect.

Brooks would oftentimes make the same analogy with the sport of basketball, and how it is dominated by young African American boys and girls who comprise roughly 75% of professional and major college rosters. Again, do the black athletes have better facilities growing up? No. Do they have better coaches? No. Are they better athletes than white kids? No. The answer, according to Brooks was simple. They grew up playing countless hours of unstructured basketball in their neighborhoods, just like he had done back in the 1940s on St. Paul's east side. That is where the passion for the game is shaped and fostered.

In the end, Brooks wanted to incorporate the "old school" methods of training with our great indoor facilities; great coaches; and great training methods of today. He would be the first to admit that we have done a good job of growing the game and that we have built a lot of beautiful arenas across the country. But in the traditional hockey hot-beds in the north and east, we need to get the kids back outdoors where they can appreciate the game and just have fun.

Brooks wanted the grow the base of the pyramid throughout the United States, and get more boys and girls interested in the sport. He also wanted them to learn the game on a grass roots basis, so that they could enjoy it on their own time, without having to always deal with parents and coaches. He saw how the lack of indoor ice time was actually hurting the game, because kids now oftentimes have to play or practice either really early in the morning or really late at night. The result is oftentimes measured in poor play, or worse yet, frustration and burn-out by players and coaches alike.

Brooks knew that serious reform would require serious rethinking. Albert Einstein once said: "You can not solve a problem from the mindset that created it," and I am sure Herbie would whole-heartedly concur. He wanted to "give the game back to the kids," and grow the game from "good to great." That is what it was all about for Herb Brooks and that will certainly always be a part of his legacy.

THE COMMON
DENOMINATORS OF SUCCESS...

"The secret of everyone who has been successful lies in the fact that they formed the habit of doing things that failures don't like to do. It's just as true as it sounds and it's just as simple as it seems. Understand right now that success is achieved by the minority and therefore is unnatural and not to be achieved by following our natural likes and dislikes, nor by being guided by our natural preferences and prejudices.

"Successful people have a purpose strong enough to make them form good habits and thus do things they don't like to do in order to accomplish the purpose they want to accomplish. This purpose, or commitment, has to do with the ultimate loyalty. It can be to preserve a tradition; uphold an ideology; or do a certain kind of work. In a sense, commitment is one's reason for living, one's 'calling.' It gives an overall direction and purpose for life. Remember it is easier to adjust to hardships of a poor living than it is to adjust ourselves to the hardships of goal setting. If you doubt me, think of the things you are willing to go without in order to avoid doing the things you don't like to do.

"All of which seems to prove that the strength which holds you to your purpose is not your own strength but the strength of your reason for living. Form good habits and become slaves unto them. Then they will evolve into your commitment and purpose for existing. For in the last analysis, your future is not going to depend on economic conditions or outside influences over which you have no control. Your future will revolve around your commitment in life.

"Make your purpose practical, but be careful not to make it logical. Make a purpose of the sentimental or emotional type. Remember needs are logical, while wants and desires are sentimental and emotional. Your needs will push you just so far...but when your needs are satisfied, they will stop pushing you. If, however, your purpose is in terms of wants or desires, then you will keep pushing long after your needs are satisfied until your desires are fulfilled."

— Herb Brooks

CH. 17) CHOOSING YOUR FAMILY OVER YOUR CAREER WILL ALWAYS BE LOOKED BACK AT AS A WISE CAREER MOVE

When the New York Rangers made Brooks a multi-million dollar offer to become their new head coach in 2003, odds-makers would have handicapped that bet as a lock. The one thing about Herb Brooks though, was that you never knew what he was going to do next. He had already committed to becoming a full-time grandpa at that point, and was not going to let down his family for any amount of money.

By now, Herbie was 65 years old and most of his friends were getting ready to retire and start spending their Winters in Florida. For all intents and purposes, life was good. Herbie had five grandchildren and was looking forward to spending as much time with them as humanly possible. He had missed out on a lot of things with his own kids and wanted to be there this time around. As for hockey, he was still working with the Penguins in scouting and as the director of player development. So, he still had his icy "fix" when he needed it. He was doing more motivational speaking, and at $15 to $20 grand a pop, why not? Yup, life was good.

Several months later, Herbie got a call he certainly wasn't expecting to get. It turned out that his old team, the New York Rangers, wanted him back. In fact, they were desperate for his services. They had a massive payroll, nearly $70 million, but couldn't make the playoffs to save their lives. They needed an inspirational leader who could take them back to the promised land; they needed somebody with an old-school, no-nonsense attitude who could whip a bunch of pampered millionaires into shape; they needed a miracle. They needed Herbie. So, they offered him a multi-million dollar multi-year deal to come back to the Big Apple and right the ship. How's that for a curve ball?

Herbie was torn. On one hand he was content to play golf, speak on the rubber chicken circuit and spend time with Patti watching their grandkids grow up. On the other hand, that was a pretty big enchilada that had just been thrown his way. He went back and forth and consult-

ed a lot of opinions along the way. In the end though, he chose to stay put and said no. He had promised his family that this was going to be their time and he was a man of his word. Plus, he just did not want to get back into the rat race and chaos of New York City. He was enjoying life and finally enjoying the fruits of his labor.

"You know, a lot of people don't realize just how close he was to accepting the Rangers job," said longtime friend and legal advisor Neil Sheehy. "He actually accepted it one evening at dinner with Louie Nanne and I at the St. Paul Hotel, but then after sleeping on it that night, decided to turn it down. I think he didn't want the stress of it all and didn't want to be alone like he was in Pittsburgh. He used to always tell me and Paul Ostby, when we were traveling on scouting trips together, that he only had so many Friday and Saturday nights left on this earth and that he didn't want to spend them with a couple of sh-- bums like us! I told him that Manhattan was a lot better than Des Moines, Dubuque, Waterloo and Grand Forks, but he still decided against it. Who knows what could've been. I think he still had the coaching bug in him, but he just couldn't make up his mind. So, he wound up spending more time with a sh-- bum like me, which, in reality, was wonderful for me. I tried to push him and pull him into doing it, but he had had enough. It was going to be family time for him and he was excited about that."

Brooks' longtime friend and former teammate, Lou Nanne, who had been helping him negotiate a contract with the Rangers, had a unique

perspective on the situation.

"Herbie was a rare individual who could talk about the game of hockey all day long," recalled Nanne. "He just loved it. He was intrigued with it; he was enamored with it; he was enchanted by it; and was genuinely interested in seeing kids get better at it. He was just absorbed with hockey, and that is what made Herbie, Herbie. He would eventually get burned out and try to get away from the game every now and then, but he would always come back. Even with the New York Rangers job, he just couldn't make up his mind as to whether or not he wanted to get back into the game or not. You just never knew with Herbie."

"That might have been his best quality and it might have been his worst, I don't know. The most consistent thing about Herb Brooks, was his inconsistency to do the things you thought he was going to do. If you thought he was going to coach team ABC, he would instead coach team XYZ. That was just his style, he always kept you guessing. It wasn't necessarily always about money either, it was just about whatever he felt was the right fit for him at that particular moment in his life."

With that difficult decision behind him, Brooks began to slow down a little bit. He tried to spend as much time as he could with his five amazing grandkids, watching their various activities, having them for sleep-overs and spoiling them with his affection. His motivational speaking career was taking off too, especially in the wake of winning the silver medal at the 2002 Winter Games. During that time Brooks had been featured on several prime time television interviews, including a nearly 10 minute segment with Tom Brokaw during the NBC Nightly News.

He had also been written up in nearly every major news publication in the country. It would open doors for Brooks with companies and organizations from coast to coast who wanted him to come speak to their employees about what it took to become a champion. As a speaker, Herb was one of the best. He was one of the most sought after celebrities out there, frequently being hired to speak to the executives of Fortune 500 companies throughout North America. There, he would speak about team building, leadership, motivation, perseverance and commitment. He would also talk about dreams, because Herbie was a dreamer. He encouraged those in attendance to believe in themselves and to follow their dreams. He spoke with a passion straight from his heart. When he was done, they would rise up in unison and applaud, pausing only long enough to wipe away their tears. Oftentimes, after listening to his presentation, many believed that they too could win a gold medal.

He was also giving back to the game, which was very important to him. He had never stopped giving back of his time and of his resources, but now he could get more involved with some of the smaller issues which had eluded him in years past. So, in addition to speaking to large corporations, Brooks also found time to speak to small youth hockey associations too. He gave generously of his time and made the effort to be there for those who needed him. He was never one to use his celebrity powers for personal gain, but he did use them from time to time to help open doors and get things done for causes near and dear to his heart.

That Summer, Brooks was enjoying himself. He was spending a lot of time gardening out in the back yard and he was spending a lot of time with his grandkids. He loved all of his grandkids dearly, but was especially looking forward to teaching the game of hockey to his daughter Kelly's twin boys. He knew that they were going to be good. Their father Marc played college hockey; their grandfather, Bob Paradise, played in the NHL back in the 1970s, and their great grandpa, Bob Dill, was a tough guy for the New York Rangers back in the 1940s. Not to mention Dill's uncles, Tommy and Mike Gibbons, who were both world champion boxers back in the 1920s. Talk about thoroughbred lineage. Herbie knew those kids were going to be tough and he was really looking forward to watching them grow up both on and off the ice.

Herbie was also enjoying playing golf, something he dearly loved. In fact, it may have been his only true vice in life. He loved everything about the game; the competition; the serenity; even the exercise. So, when civic and charitable organizations called to see if he could make appearances at their celebrity golf tournaments, well, that was like killing two birds with one stone in his eyes. What could be better than spending a beautiful Summer day outside with your old pals, while still helping out a good cause. Yes, life was good.

In August, Herbie got asked to play in the U.S. Hockey Hall of Fame Celebrity Golf Classic, up at Giant's Ridge Golf Course in Biwabik, Minn. He loved that particular golf course and was really looking forward to spending the weekend with some of his dearest friends up on the Iron Range. He would spend the weekend with his buddies playing golf, telling stories and catching up on old times. And, he would be doing his part to promote the growth of American hockey. Herbie was an inductee of the Hall of Fame and was always willing to do whatever he could to help them out.

On the morning of Monday, August 13th, Herbie arrived at the golf course ready to go. He had spent the weekend at his old friend John Mayasich's cabin and was having a ball seeing all his old friends. He would only be able to play golf for a few hours though, due to the fact that he had to drive back to the Twin Cities later that day in order to catch a flight to Chicago, where he had a speaking engagement that evening.

Finally, after 11 holes, and a great day on the course, Herbie had to take off. It had been a wonderful morning, but he had to honor his prior commitments. With that, he packed up and headed back to his home, just north of St. Paul in White Bear Lake. Sadly and tragically, however, Herbie never made it. On the afternoon of August 11, 2003, Herb Brooks died in a one car accident just north of the Twin Cities near the intersections of Interstates 35W and 35E, by the suburb of Forest Lake. His vehicle had veered off the road and overturned; he was killed instantly. He was just 66 years old.

CH. 18) A LEGEND WITH A
TRULY LASTING LEGACY

Herb Brooks made a difference in his lifetime and made sure to leave an enduring legacy behind. He had a passion for the game of hockey and luckily for us, through that medium he was able to change the world. What's your passion? What are your dreams? Who will carry your torch for you when you are gone?   What would your legacy be if your life ended tomorrow? Life is short, define it; own it; and live it the way Herb Brooks did. That is my challenge to you. And maybe, just maybe, you too will be inspired to create your own miracle.

The entire nation was shocked and saddened by the horrible news. All of the national news organizations, from CNN to FOX, went to live feeds of the accident. That evening, every major news outlet ran it as the lead story of their broadcasts. It was a huge story, and not just in the world of sports either. Herb Brooks had been a national hero, and was being remembered as such. In Minnesota, meanwhile, where Brooks was like royalty, it was a day that would never be forgotten. Words couldn't describe the collective mood of the citizens of the Land of 10,000 Lakes, where sadness and grief consumed nearly everybody's thoughts and prayers.

The outpouring of emotion came from all walks of life. "He was a consummate teacher, an unparalleled motivator and an unquestioned innovator," said NHL Commissioner Gary Bettman. "His candle burned out much too soon, but his success will live on in the people he touched," noted USA Hockey Chairman Walter Bush. And then there was this reaction from Minnesota Governor Tim Pawlenty, a well-known hockey fanatic. "My gut reaction is Minnesota lost its head coach today. Herb Brooks was a Minnesota legend, a Minnesota treasure."

From there, people reflected on what Herbie had meant to them, and about his legacy. Longtime friend and former Bemidji State University head coach Bob Peters might have said it best: "There is an old quote that I think sums up Herbie pretty well, and it reads: 'He was willing to do what had to be done, sacrifice what had to be sacrificed and give what he had to give.' That was Herbie to me, he was just that kind of a person. He was a missionary and an apostle. I am going to miss him and hockey is going to miss him."

Herb's funeral was a venerable who's who of the hockey world, with several thousand dignitaries, politicians, family members, friends, coaches and fans alike, all coming out to pay their respects to one of the

true patriarchs of the game. Brooks' body was viewed in an open casket, covered with an assortment of brightly colored cards and drawings from his grandchildren. Next to him were a single rose and a small American flag. The funeral mass began with a lone bagpiper playing *"Amazing Grace,"* and ended with the singing of *"The Battle Hymn of the Republic."* In typical Herbie fashion, the Mass was a wonderful mix of the rich and famous alongside the blue-collar and poor.

"I remember speaking at his funeral and just looking up through those thousands of people and seeing so many spheres of life," recalled longtime friend Larry Hendrickson. "You could see guys in nice Italian suits, and you could see guys in golf shirts and jeans. There were all races and religions, that was the impact he had. He crossed borders and touched everybody in some way. I mean he could speak to executives from IBM one day at a speaking junket, and speak to a guy on the street the next. That was just natural for him and that is what made him so unique.

"I remember being at the wake, the day before his funeral, and going through the line to pay my respects. I saw this kid go through the line by himself and then went back to the pews and started crying. I didn't think anything of it at the time, but about 45 minutes later I saw the kid still back there crying. So, I went over to talk to him. I introduced myself and told him that I knew he felt bad and just wanted to see if he was OK. I asked him if he wanted to talk about it.

"The kid then proceeded to tell me that one day he was having breakfast at a restaurant and that at the time he was going through a tough time and was going to drop out of school. So, he sees Herbie sitting there eating, and he goes up to him and introduces himself to him. He said 'Mr. Brooks, I was wondering if I could just meet you.' Herbie says, 'sure, sit down and have breakfast with me.' Well anyway, they got talking for an hour and he said by the time they were done the kid was total-

"THE NAME ON THE FRONT OF THE SWEATER IS MUCH MORE IMPORTANT THAN THE NAME ON THE BACK."

Just a few weeks before Herbie died, I had asked him if he would write the foreword for a coffee table book which I had just written entitled *"Legends & Legacies: Celebrating a Century of Minnesota Coaches."* In it I asked him how he would want to be remembered when it was all said and done. Ironically, this was what he had to say: *"He sacrificed for the unknown and had truly piece of mind. You know, I have always felt strongly about the name on the front of the sweater being much more important than the name on the back. They'll forget about individuals in this world, but they'll always remember the teams. That's how I want to be remembered."*

ly committed to going back to school and getting his life back on track. He said that out of nowhere, Herbie took the time for him and really made a difference in his life. And, by the way, he said Herbie even bought him breakfast. I mean that was Herbie to a tee."

Former Gopher Bill Butters and 1980 Olympian Mike Eruzione each gave wonderful eulogies in his honor. Butters spoke from his heart, while Eruzione kept it light: "Right now, Herbie is saying to God, 'I don't like the style of your team. We should change it...' " Noted St. Paul Pioneer Press scribe Tom Powers might have said it best following Eruzione's hilarious one-liner: "My money is on Herb, and I wouldn't be surprised if, in a few months, we all are attending church on Tuesdays and the 10 Commandments have been whittled to six or seven."

Butters also read from a piece that Neil Sheehy had written about his old friend: "Coach, mentor, teacher, counselor, confidante, motivator, friend — Herb Brooks was many things to many people and what he shared with every one of us was magical. His magic was captured by a nation through a hockey game in 1980, but those of us who knew him and lived with him experienced his character and his magic with each passing moment shared with him. Herb Brooks is one of those few truly remarkable people who walked this earth among us. His brilliance as a man and in hockey was only surpassed by his uncompromising principles from which he could never waiver, even to his own peril. Without hesitation, he always told us where he stood, which is why we followed. Simple yet complex, bullheaded yet compassionate, famous yet never forgot his roots, Herb Brooks impacted our lives as he gave of himself daily. He challenged us not to be ordinary, but to make a difference in our lives and become extraordinary"

Then, in a lighter moment, Reverend John Malone spoke of Herbie's East Side roots: "I have a message for the East Siders here," he said, "and this is coming from someone who grew up three doors down from the old Harding High School. Consider just some of the accomplishments of Herb Brooks, as a hockey player at the University of Minnesota and for two Olympic teams, coach of three Gopher national championship teams, coach of U.S. Olympic hockey teams that won the 1980 gold medal and 2002 silver and as a professional coach. Incredible. But for a moment, imagine if he had lived on the right side of the East Side and gone to Harding, not Johnson. It boggles the imagination!" The church erupted with laughter. Even Herbie would've cracked a smile at that one.

Malone also likened Brooks' coaching of the overachieving 1980 team to a biblical passage: "Most miracles are dreams made manifest," Malone said. "Herbie had a dream. The players had a dream. If we could all dream ... and do our best, we could make this a better world. It's within our reach; it's within God's reach."

Afterwards, honorary pall bearers hoisting hockey sticks saluted Herbie as he left the opulent St. Paul Cathedral. Meanwhile, high above in the sky, a formation of World War II vintage airplanes flew overhead in his honor. There wasn't a dry eye in sight as the casket was taken down the steps and carried away for a private burial at Roselawn Cemetery in St. Paul.

As a player and coach, Herbie wanted to be remembered as someone who sacrificed for the unknown and truly had piece of mind. And, he always felt strongly about the name on the front of the jersey being much more important than the name on the back — which summed him up to a tee. As a person, however, Herbie wanted to be remembered much differently. He wanted to be known as just a "regular guy" who wasn't any better than anybody else. He would also want to be remembered for being a hard worker who was always there for those who needed him. Herbie's longtime friend and next-door neighbor, Bob Rink, concurred.

"We were just two 65-year-old guys who had raised their families together and were on to bigger and better things in life," said Rink. "You know, I was so amazed being at his funeral and seeing all the different people who were there, from the rich to the gifted to the famous. And then realizing that his best friend, of all those thousands of people, was LeRoy Houle, who trims trees. That was his best friend. That speaks volumes of who Herb Brooks was."

"I remember one day I saw Herb in the garage and he had some old clothes and boots on and as I was leaving for work. I said, 'boy you are getting an early start today.' He said, 'Yeah, LeRoy has a big project going on and can't get anybody to help him so I am going to work for him for a couple of weeks.' Herb Brooks, the famous coach and celebrity, went to work, probably for nothing I am sure, for two weeks trimming trees for LeRoy Houle. That is the kind of person Herb Brooks was. I have known a lot of famous and successful people over the years, and believe me, they wouldn't think twice about doing that. They would make a phone call or two to try to find somebody to help LeRoy. But Herb knew that his friend needed help and he was there for him. So, he put on his boots and went to work. That was the way he lived his life. He would do that for anybody. Yet, he was this tough guy who would holler at the refs during big games and things like that. Then, you would see him walking this little white dog down the street. So, there was an entirely different side of Herb Brooks that most people didn't know about. He was just a special person."

Another person who had a unique perspective on Brooks' pension for being "the common man," was 1976 Gopher team captain, Pat Phippen. "You know, Herbie was just a common guy who never let his ego get the better of him," said Phippen. "I actually ran into him at a celebrity golf tournament just a couple of weeks before the accident. Well, at the first tee, an announcer would introduce every player, followed by where they were a member at. So, for instance he would say: 'Lou Nanne: Spring Hill,' and so and so, from Interlachen Country Club, and so on. All of the celebrities were members of really nice, expensive courses. Well, they finally get around to introducing Herbie and the announcer says 'Herb Brooks: Shadow Ridge.' Shadow Ridge? Where was Shadow Ridge, it must be pretty exclusive people thought.

164

Well, little did anybody know, but Shadow Ridge was his driving range! That was Herbie."

"Even after the Olympics, when he was a big-time celebrity, he used to be in a pool league with the local patrons at Kelly's Bar in this little town of Centerville. He was just one of the guys. What can you say, the guy never forgot his roots. He liked hanging around guys like that. I mean look at the guys who were at the 'U' when I was there, not one of them came from a dime. Herbie could relate to them and went after those kids who were blue collar workers, much like he was."

Beneath his hardened exterior, Brooks was an extremely compassionate and caring person. While he sometimes had a hard time expressing those feeling, those who knew him best felt it when it mattered most.

"Herbie touched my life on so many levels and for so many years," said former Gopher Joe Micheletti. "He really became like a part of our family. You know, when my father died, we were at the wake up in Hibbing. Well, there was a classic Minnesota blizzard going on outside at the time, but Herb still made the four hour trip up to be there for us. Then, when my mother died, Herb came from a scouting trip in Montreal to be at that funeral as well. We really appreciated that. So, he has meant a great deal to me and my family and I just can't say enough nice things about Herb Brooks. He was such a decent, wonderful human being. The thing that stands out though, is the way he cared for people."

Brooks also took the time to let people know how he felt about them. He was a great communicator. He wasn't always vocal about his thoughts though, and that is what made him so unique. One of things he was most known for were his handwritten notes. He wasn't a computer guy and much preferred the old school way of expressing himself. In today's high-tech instant-message e-mail world, Brooks was truly a throwback. And that is what made him so special to so many different people.

"The thing I will remember most about him was that whenever something happened, good or bad, in someone's life, they always got a note from Herbie," recalled former North Star & current Wild radio analyst, Tommy Reid. "He never forgot to send you a little note to congratulate you or to say some kind words about you. He did that with so many people and I tell you, when you got a note from Herbie it was really something special. Those little things made such an impact on people's lives."

"You know, it was the little things with Herb that made such a difference," added former University of Wisconsin head coach, Jeff Sauer. "I remember a few days after I won the national championship with Wisconsin in 1990, I got a really nice note from Herbie telling me what a great job I did and that he hoped I had a great Summer. Then, a few years back when my father died, who shows up? Herbie. I really appreciated that so much. We were both St. Paul guys, and we respected each other a great deal. He was just such a thoughtful person and I thought the world of him. He was one of those guys who was bigger than life."

Herbie tried to treat everybody with respect, especially the behind the scenes guys who didn't always get the credit he felt they deserved. He made it a point to treat those people right, and that kindness and loyalty was always appreciated and reciprocated, usually ten times over.

"Herbie always considered himself to be a lunch pail kind of a guy," said Gary Smith, who served as the team trainer under Brooks at Minnesota and on the 1980 U.S. Olympic team. "He always took care of the little people — the bus drivers, equipment managers, trainers, janitors or what have you. He had a tremendous compassion for the job that they did and appreciated them as human beings. I remember during the Olympics sometimes we would be in the locker room hanging gear until like two or three in the morning, and when we got back to the hotel there would be sandwiches there waiting for us with a nice note from Herb. He just appreciated the little things, and as a result we all wanted to do our best for him."

"He gave us a lot of responsibility too. I just did whatever I could to help out the team. I remember every now and then if we were tired and needed a rest, I would hop over the boards and tell the ref that one of our guys had lost a contact lens. So, I would be down on all fours looking and looking and finally I would spit out a lens that I had had in my mouth the entire time, eventually picking it up off the ice for him to see. Little things like that went a long way and Herb appreciated that stuff. You know, sometimes the fringe people get left behind with big name coaches and what not, but not with Herbie. We were just as important to him as his top centerman, or at least that was how he made us feel."

Gary Gambucci, a former Gopher and teammate of Brooks' on two U.S. National teams, had his own unique perspective about the secrets of his old friend's success: "He just loved hockey and always wanted to improve the game for the next generation of kids," said Gambucci. "That was what Herbie was all about. He wanted to make better people

JUST A GUY FROM THE EAST SIDE...

The historic St. Paul Hotel has a wall of fame which features famous Minnesotans on it who are now deceased. On it are pictures of people such as Judy Garland, Hubert Humphrey and F. Scott Fitzgerald, among others. Each picture lists the person's name, what they did, their birth and death dates, and then one line about them to sum up their life. As for Herbie's plaque, underneath *"HOCKEY LEGEND,"* it reads: *"JUST A GUY FROM THE EAST SIDE..."*. That really kind of says it all because he truly never forgot his roots and was very proud of where he came from.

out of everybody. You didn't have to like him when you were playing for him, but when you were done, that was when you realized what he was trying to accomplish. He was hard on his kids, and even tougher on his superstars, because he knew that they had more to give. He just always wanted to raise the bar for everybody, and that was why the guy was so successful."

As for Brook's legacy? It will be many things to many people. It is alive and well, however, as the sport of hockey continues to grow and expand throughout the world. That was his cause; his mission; to grow the game the right way, with respect, dignity and passion. He did just like John Mariucci had done before him, he gave back to the sport and championed causes which were near and dear to his heart. He used his political clout to get things done and was able to encourage communities to build more arenas and get more young boys and girls playing the game. He also encouraged former players to come home after their playing days and to pay it forward, to get into youth coaching and to keep the "success breeds success" model going for future generations. He also inspired a younger generation who grew up wanting to become coaches and teachers as well.

"Herb was the best coach that I ever had," said former 1980 U.S. Olympian & current St. John's University head coach, John Harrington. "He was so good with motivational things, tactical things, strategy, preparation and hard work. There was just nobody like him. As for me, I have been coaching college hockey for more than 20 years now, and I draw much of my style from him. I know that from playing for him on the Olympic team that if my teams now work hard, good things will happen and that sometimes dreams can come true."

"The Miracle was something that could only have happened if a certain coach had put a certain team in that exact position to be able to pull off something that was seemingly unattainable at the time," recalled famed TV announcer Al Michaels. " Herb Brooks was that coach and he was able to accomplish things that most humans couldn't dream of. There have been very few men or women in history, not just sports history, who have had that ability. Luckily for us, Herb had that ability. He was truly a one of a kind."

As for his honors and accolades, there are many. Throughout his career Herb earned great recognition both individually and for his country. He has been inducted into the Olympic Hall of Fame, the U.S. Hockey Hall of Fame, the International Ice Hockey Hall of Fame, and the University of Minnesota and the State of Minnesota Halls of Fames. In addition, he also received the coveted Lester Patrick Award for his contributions to American hockey. Furthermore, in the Summer of 2006, Brooks received hockey's highest honor when it was announced that he had been selected for induction into the Hockey Hall of Fame, in Toronto. He is one of just a handful of Americans ever to be enshrined. Lastly, on February 23, 2005, at a special 25th Anniversary celebration in Lake Placid, the rink where Brooks coached the U.S. Olympic hockey team to its stunning gold-medal victory a quarter century earlier, was renamed as "Herb Brooks Arena" in his honor.

Perhaps the most visible tribute, however, came in 2004 when Disney released the movie "Miracle," which chronicled the 1980 U.S. Olympic team through Herbie's eyes. The reviews were great and hockey fans everywhere marveled at its authenticity. It instantly became a "classic" for fans and teams alike who would watch it over and over to get really psyched up before a big game.

Famed actor Kurt Russell starred as Herb in the movie and really nailed it. From the accent to the way he skated to how he even chewed his gum, it was incredible. Patti used to tease Herbie that she wished she could have played herself in the movie, starring opposite Kurt. Herb said he would go along with it if he could, in turn, have a love scene with Russell's longtime companion, Goldie Hawn. Needless to say, actress Patricia Clarkson got the role of Patti. It was a nice try though!

The movie was infinitely better than the original "Miracle on Ice" movie which came out in the early '80s and starred Karl Malden, who might have been in his 70s at the time. Herbie's buddies used to tease him that he had gotten a lot younger and a lot better looking all those years later when the new movie came out. He wholeheartedly agreed.

It is interesting to note that actor Tom Hanks was originally considered for the role of Herb, but Russell actually lobbied for it. You see, Herbie had met the actor a few years earlier when he was scouting for Pittsburgh and had taken a look at Russell's son, Wyatt, a goaltender who was playing Junior hockey in Vancouver at the time. Herbie and Kurt hit it off and became friends. Herbie then worked as a consultant during the making of the movie, giving Russell a lot of valuable feedback along the way. While Herbie did not get to see the final product at the theater, as the last line of the movie stated, it just didn't matter, "because he lived it."

Kurt Russell as Herbie in the movie "Miracle"

The movie also brought Brooks' legend to a whole new generation of fans. "It showed people he was an extremely dedicated individual," said Dan Brooks. "He was so driven. He worked so tirelessly, and he had an amazing goal he accomplished through hard work. His greatest legacy is the lesson that if you believe, you can achieve anything you want in life."

"The Miracle is something that has lasted for over a quarter of a century, and in fact, it's lore just continues to grow," recalled famed TV announcer Al Michaels. "Even now, all these years later, when people watch the movie 'Miracle,' they feel the same way. It is amazing just how many teams have watched that movie before their biggest games too. I hear that from NFL coaches all the time. They show it to their players on Saturday nights before their games that next morning to get them fired up and inspired. And it works. It is a great movie and it really capsulizes those events in an incredible way. Plus, it is neat to see a whole new generation of kids being able to watch it and learn all about it. It's historic."

One of our nation's most charismatic and innovative coaches, Herb Brooks was a true American hero. Whether he was competing in the business world, on the ice, or even on the diamond of a world championship fast-pitch softball team, he took the same no-nonsense attitude and intensity to whatever he did, and that's why he was so successful. His legacy will live on forever in the youth of America as they continue to enjoy the fruits of his lifetime commitment to bettering the game. In the world of hockey coaching, no one was larger than Herb Brooks. He was simply the best of the best; an icon; and he is dearly missed.

As it has been said so many times, Herb never forgot where he came from and was always proud of his east side heritage. Whether he was enjoying a burger and talking hockey at Serlin's Cafe, or having a cold one with his high school pals at Yarusso's, Brooks stayed true to his colorful working-class neighborhood roots. In St. Paul, Herbie was more than royalty, but if you asked him, he would just say that he was a "Joe Six-Pack" from Payne Avenue.

As a motivator, nobody was better than Brooks. He could get people's attention. That's why Democrats and Republicans alike tried to get him to run for political office on more than one occasion over the years. Whether it was in sports or in life, you just never knew what you were going to get with him either. Depending upon his mood, he could be a teacher, coach, psychologist, orator, tactician, philosopher, politician, or even a stand-up comedian. Regardless, he made sure that his boys played to their own individual potentials. Everybody had a role on his teams and he would convince each player that their role was the most important one for the team's success. Without them performing their role, the team would fail. More importantly, they would be letting their teammates down, which to Brooks was even worse than losing.

Herbie was tough, controversial and said whatever was on his mind, whenever he wanted. He was so principled, so determined and so passionate about the causes that he believed in, that once he got something in his head, it was going to get done — no matter what. That was Herbie. In fact, looking back at Al Michael's notorious last second call from the game against the Soviets, *"Do you believe in miracles?... Yes!"* — one can only assume that Herb probably didn't. That's right. Sure, he was a dreamer, but there were no short-cuts or divine interventions for this guy. It was all about hard work, commitment and passion. And luckily for us his obsession was hockey, a medium through which he changed the face of history.

To honor Brooks, there was a statue erected of him in St. Paul's Rice Park, across the way from another St. Paul icon, writer F. Scott Fitzgerald. Ironically, it was Fitzgerald who wrote the now famous line: *"Show me a hero and I will show you a tragedy."* That was Herbie. Gone from this earth, Herb Brooks has truly earned his place in sports immortality. You will be dearly missed.

The Brooks Grandchildren

DAN BROOKS' MEMORIES
OF HIS FATHER...

"My dad wasn't a warm, touchy-feely kind of a guy," said Dan. "He didn't wear his emotions on his sleeve. He kept things pretty close to the vest. He didn't like people to see him hugging and kissing anybody either. But, that all changed with the grandkids. He was still pretty discrete about it though, and would only kiss the kids when he thought nobody was looking. It was actually pretty funny to see him that affectionate with them. It was definitely a new emotion for him, and one our family certainly welcomed."

"He loved his grandkids very much, he truly did. They made him laugh and they made him relax a little bit, both things my father needed more of in his life. He always wanted them around too. He would say to my mom 'call Danny and tell him to have Grace sleep over here tonight...'. Stuff like that was pretty funny. My mom is the ultimate grandma and together they spoiled all of the kids rotten. I know that he was particularly looking forward to watching his two grandsons grow up with hockey. Those two kids are kind of wild and they are tough, so we all figure that they are going to be really good players. It's just sad that he won't get to see any of the kids grow up.

"People express their love in different ways and my dad wasn't overly affectionate by any means. Rather, he was a great provider. He took care of us. I mean he would go down to the basement when I wasn't around and make sure that my hockey equipment was all hung up so that it dried out properly. He did stuff like that, behind the scenes, to take care of you without you even knowing it. He wanted to make sure that no mold grew on my elbow pads and that my skate blades were dry and didn't rust. It was little things like that which made him happy. He was odd that way, but that was how he showed his love to us.

"As for the oddities of my father? There were many. For starters, he loved basements and garages. He was notorious for just showing up at my house, unbeknownst to me of course, and organizing my garage. He would bring over tools for me and get them all organized, later telling me that I might need them for various future projects that I may decide to partake in. It was hilarious. I remember one time he came over and was rummaging around my basement. I have a pretty big house with a lot of storage rooms down there, and on this particular day he had decided to commandeer one of those rooms to make me a work bench. I said 'Dad, please, I do not need or want, for that matter, a work bench.' I am a stock broker for God's sake. I pay people, experts in their craft, to do that kind of work for me. What am I going to do, come home from a long day at work and build a bird house? Come on, I have no desire whatsoever to build anything, none. That is why I work as hard as I do at my job, so I don't have to have a work bench. I don't even cut my own grass, which was another thing that my father could just not understand.

"My father was determined to build me a work bench though, and not just a Menards cheap-o either, this one was going to be top of the line complete with a vice and all the bells and whistles. Finally, I just told him, 'Dad, save your time and money, I do not want you to build me a work bench.' Well, he didn't care, he went off to Home Depot and loaded up on tools and God knows what. He hauled it all over here and built this giant thing down there. I appreciated what he did, but I never got into it the way he had hoped.

"The last time I saw my dad alive, it was about 10 days before the accident, and he came over to drop off two brand new saw horses for me. I remember saying to him 'Dad, what in the hell am I going to do with these?' He just figured that they should be a part of my new work bench ensemble, and took it upon himself to keep me stocked up with all the necessary tools that I may need, just in case a natural disaster hit or something. The sad part of it now is that all of that stuff, his tools and things that he used to build it, are still down in that room. His big bag of power tools is still sitting in there and whenever I walk by it I just think of him. It's like a museum down there. I don't know what to do with all of that stuff but I just can't seem to bring myself to clean it up."

"As for his vices? That was easy, he loved gardening and landscaping. He would spend thousands and thousands of dollars on hostas and trees. He loved that stuff. Being out there with the plants and shrubs, that was his sanctuary. My sister used to be out there with him, that was their thing. My dad and I bonded through hockey, whereas those guys spent time together gardening instead. As a result, Kelly loves to garden to this day, and I pay a guy to mow my lawn and do my landscaping. Go figure.

"My dad was a pretty focused guy. When he was into hockey, that was it. Then, when he was gardening or building something, that was his entire focus. It was like when he was doing one, the other was completely out of mind, and visa versa. Yet, the two had to exist for him to survive. He needed to be able to get away from the grind of coaching by being able to plant shrubs. Then, when he was planting shrubs, he was thinking and planning about how he could coach better and come up with different strategies.

"He also loved to golf and he loved to watch sports on TV. He was a big sports fan, he really was. And, like most Minnesotans, he liked watching the Vikings on Sundays. I remember watching Twins games with him during the Summers when I was in high school too. We would spend the day out on the lake and then, after cleaning up, we would sit down and watch the ballgame together. Those were great memories. He also loved watching the Olympic sports too, like gymnastics, which he really enjoyed for some reason. Playoff hockey was the ultimate though. My dad and Warren Strelow would get together in the Spring, if they were both in town, and watch the Stanley Cup games religiously. He would be at Warren's house every single night watching it. I would go with him and we had a ball, it was great to watch that stuff with my dad and to hear his commentary. He and Warren would hang out and give each other sh--, it was awesome.

"As for the life lessons I learned from my father, there were many. I learned so much from my dad over the years, I really did. One of the biggest things about my dad was the fact that he was so well prepared for everything he did. He was so thorough and methodical about every little detail, he just did not like to leave anything to chance. He also expected everyone to do the same, which was difficult at times for those around him. I will say this about him though, he never lost a game because he was outworked or unprepared. He was a machine, he really was. I think that is what I learned the most from him, the value of hard work. I am that way in my own business now and pride myself on being a tireless worker and planner. I remember, my dad had one very simple saying that he told me before I started college at the University of Denver. He said to me 'be the first one on the ice, the last one to leave and keep your mouth shut.' That was it, very simple and to the point, just like my dad. Well, I did, and I made the team. So, I applied that same theory to my life in whatever I did.

"Maybe the biggest thing I will take away from my dad was that he was always so respectful of the 'little people.' I don't mean that term in a derogatory way whatsoever, I just mean he always made time for the janitors, the equipment managers, the bus drivers and the maintenance workers. My dad was a pretty famous guy. He was on the *Tonight Show*, he was friends with the President, he rubbed elbows with movie stars and celebrities, and he was the NHL Coach of the Year. He had it all. Yet, he much preferred to hang out with the 'little people.' Whenever he got free stuff from companies or what not, he always gave it away to those people. He never felt that he was better than them.

"Even when he was at various functions with celebrities and dignitaries, he would oftentimes be out back talking to the janitors or the cooks. That was just who he felt most comfortable with I think. He never forgot his roots on the east side of St. Paul and I really respect him for that. He also didn't care that much about material things. A lot of his friends and colleagues drove fancy cars, belonged to posh country clubs and traveled the world, but that stuff didn't matter to him. He had a close bond with the east side of St. Paul and chose to live his life much more modestly than he certainly could have.

"He loved the blue collar guy, the underdog, that was just part of his soul I think. I remember back about 10 years ago, I was back from college and working. I joined Midland Hills Country Club and somehow talked my father into joining as well. He loved to golf with a passion, but being a member of a country club wasn't big with him. He just wasn't a part of that whole social/economic thing that went along with being a member of a snooty club. So, I met him one Saturday morning out there for a round of golf. I showed up and it was real early in the morning, so I parked right out in front, like in the first stall. I started looking around for my dad, but I didn't see him. Then, I looked way down, like a couple hundred yards away, where the maintenance guys and groundskeepers parked, and I saw his old beat up pick-up truck. So, I asked him why he parked all the way down there and he said that he was just too embarrassed to have all of the big-shot members see his old truck and that they might laugh. He said he just liked to be with the grounds crew guys, where he felt more at home.

"My dad just really liked to associate himself with the blue collar people that he identified most with. I think that was evident at his funeral when so many down and out people showed up to pay their respects to him. That part of him is real important to me now. One image that I will always remember from the funeral, was as we were leaving the cathedral and walking with the pall-bearers down the steps and over to the limousines. When we got down the hill I saw this guy, a truly poor soul, with his shoes untied and his Twins hat on crooked. He had like five programs from the funeral in his hand and he was just standing there at full attention, saluting my dad and crying as we walked by. It was sort of like that image of JFK Jr. at his dad's funeral, and that image of this down-and out-guy to me was just so poignant. It totally captured the moment of what my dad was all about.

"My dad's best friend was LeRoy Houle, a tree trimmer and land-scaper who he met after the 1980 Olympics, and I think that LeRoy per-sonified the guy my dad wanted to be. He is just a very simple, blue collar guy, and my dad just loved him. We all love him, he is just the greatest guy. I mean for my dad, all the stuff that came along with being who he was, like the hob-knobbing with the big-wigs and the public speaking, that was just something that he did out of obligation. He was very loyal and that was all stuff that came along with being a celebrity. He did it because it went along with the territory, but deep down, my dad would much rather have been out working in the yard with LeRoy, and then having a beer and relaxing. Sure, he could hob-knob at the country clubs with the best of them, but that was not who he was. Really, even to this day, if Mario Lemieux or Wayne Gretzky walked into our house to pay their respects to my dad, I would be very impressed and in awe of them, but if LeRoy walked in I would cry like a baby. He is just that type of person and our family loves him.

"I would have to say that the biggest thrill I got out of all of the events that I was asked to speak at after he died was going back to St. Paul Johnson High School to receive his award for being inducted into their hall of fame. Seeing all of the people from the east side, and what my dad meant to them, really moved me. I also got a big kick out of going to his Mancini's Hall of Fame induction over on West Seventh Street, too. Believe it or not, I enjoyed those two events more than any of the others. Sure, it is fun to hobnob with the celebrities and beautiful people at the bigger hall of fame inductions and at the Hollywood movie screening, but the stuff in St. Paul is what really matters. I am sure my dad would feel the same."

"As for what my dad meant to me? He meant the world to me. "My father was sort of a two-tiered person. He was obviously a father who tried to raise me the best that he could by teaching me lessons in life. Then, he was also another person in that he was my idol, and I was a fan of his. I mean I grew up loving the sport of hockey; just loving the Gophers, the Olympic team and the New York Rangers. So, I was a fan of his and a fan of his teams. It was kind of a weird relationship some-times. I mean it would be like if you grew up loving baseball in Minnesota and idolizing Kirby Puckett and Rod Carew, only they told you what time you had to be home at night. So, being a sports fan I real-ly looked up to my dad, which made it tough sometimes. But, it was a really unique experience and I wouldn't have traded it for the world. I got to live every win and loss, just like my dad. So, when the Gophers won, I was on top of the world, but if they lost, I couldn't get out of bed the next day — just like my dad. I just experienced every emotion their was as a kid, through my dad's teams. You know, if your father was an accountant, or a lawyer or a teacher, you just didn't have those type of emotions, so that was unique, but special at the same time.

"I look back and I really appreciate my dad. I mean how many kids can say that their dad was their hero? I don't know, but I certainly did. It was such an honor to be his son and the memories that I have of him mean more to me than almost anything in the world. My dad gave me so much and I just hope that I can be as good a father to my own kids as he was to me. I was lucky. I got to see the world through hockey and I got to be with my dad for every step of the way. That was an amazing upbringing and I look back at it now just in awe. To be a youth hockey player and to be able to hang out in the locker rooms of the Gophers, Olympians and New York Rangers, wow, what can you say? It was amazing. I think I was the luckiest kid in the world for that 15 year period when I followed my dad, literally, around the world.

"My dad was all about winning. He was so competitive. He wanted to win everything he did so badly. He would just do anything and everything he could to plan and prepare in order to achieve that goal. He lived a very disciplined life and stayed extremely organized so that he didn't have to take his eyes off of his dreams and aspirations. Winning was what he was all about, both on and off the ice.

"He was just a gamer. He loved pressure and thrived under pressure. While most people got nervous over a test at school or over a big game, or what have you, my dad always used to say that tests and games were the fun parts, because you could just go out there and react. The hard part was in the preparation and the practicing that all went into it prior to that. My dad couldn't understand people who panicked under pressure and didn't act up to their true abilities. He was just always prepared, no matter what he did. I remember what Steve Ulseth, a former player of his with the Gophers, once told me. He said that guys couldn't stand him (Herbie) during the week of practice because he was so tough on them. But then, when they were in the national championship game, and it was 3-2 late in the third period, and they looked back behind the bench and saw my dad, calm and collected, leading them, they thanked their lucky stars that it was him back there and not somebody else. Preparation was the utmost thing to him and I think his players totally respected that.

"I witnessed first hand a lot of the reverse psychology and motivational tactics that he used on his players to achieve those goals too. He was tough, really tough. It was amazing. Quite frankly, a lot of his players were scared to death of him. Fear was a tactic he used to get his guys motivated and I can tell you first hand, it worked. Even the biggest badasses on his teams feared him. Every one of them. He commanded their attention and he earned their respect. He was a master motivator, no question about it.

"So, to bring that full circle with me, I really try to live by that same adage of never forgetting my roots and to always be respectful to the 'real people' around me, regardless of who they are or where they come from. That was certainly one of the most important lessons I learned from him, no question. I know that my dad loved me and I know that he knew that I loved him deeply. I had a great life with him and the memories I have, no one can take away from me. Not a day goes by that I don't think of him."

ABOUT THE AUTHOR

Ross Bernstein is the best-selling author of nearly 50 sports books and has appeared on thousands of TV and radio programs over his career, including CNN, NPR and ESPN, as well as on the covers of the Wall Street Journal, New York Times and USA Today. As an internationally recognized motivational keynote speaker, Ross uses inspirational sports stories as a metaphor for life and for business to energize and connect his audiences — challenging them to not just be ordinary, but to make a difference and be extraordinary.

From groups ranging in size from 40 to 4,000, Ross regularly speaks to corporations, sales teams and trade associations from coast to coast and his action-packed keynotes are inspirational, memorable and fun. His PowerPoint presentations feature hundreds of huge color photos which are chock full of poignant stories, practical wisdom and valuable take-aways that audience members can bring back to the office and start applying immediately. As a conference opener, Ross sets the tone right out of the gates with his high energy and engaging stories; while as a closer he leaves attendees energized, inspired and ready to get back to work.

Ross offers a couple of very popular keynote programs: *"When it Comes to Team Building, Leadership & Motivation... Do You Believe in Miracles?"* is all about the inspirational legacy of Herb Brooks. To honor his friend and mentor, Ross speaks about the influence Brooks had on the world of sports, his unorthodox leadership style, and about the impact of the now legendary "Miracle on Ice," which will forever live on as one of the greatest moments in the history of sports. Putting many of the life-lessons and ideologies he learned from the fiery coach into a practical business application, Ross' presentation aims to inspire others to follow their dreams and maybe, just maybe, even create their own miracles. In addition, *"The Champion's Code: Life Lessons of Values & Integrity from the Sports World to the Business World"* is all about the DNA of champions, and about how they differ from athletes — both on and off the field.

Ross and his wife Sara have one daughter and presently reside in Eagan, Minn. Ross also currently serves as the President of the Board of Directors of the Herb Brooks Foundation, a cause that is truly near and dear to his heart.

Ross Bernstein

www.rossbernsteinspeaking.com